"Many of us have been hurt by religious institutions and nonsensical theologies, and we need new language, images, and stories. Brandon Evans offers something beautiful in his road trip parable. It reminds me that when love is central, everything else makes sense."

—Thomas Jay Oord, author of *God Can't* and other books

"Brandon Evans has written a debut novel that is as heartfelt as it is timely. *The Parable of the Road* carries the weight of grief and the levity of humor, and Evans knows how to tell the truth about loss, love, and anger without turning away from tenderness. For readers who are deconstructing, and for evangelicals willing to see the harm done in God's name, this story offers an honest mirror and a hopeful alternative."

—Michael Joseph Brennan, Theodivergent writer and podcast host, author of *Flourish: An Open and Relational Queer Theology*

"Anyone who has wandered through their own journey of spiritual relocation and persistent questioning will find *The Parable of the Road* to be a refreshing companion that encourages and invites honest reflection."

—Tracy L. Tucker ThD, BCC, CT, Hospice Chaplain, author of *Can We Talk About Death? An Open and Relational Vision*

"Brandon Evans' *The Parable of the Road* has so much to offer. I was immediately drawn in by the humor. As I read, the characters came to life and I recognized my story reflected in theirs. After finishing, it seems as though I can see myself and others a little more clearly. If you need more of the good, the true, and the beautiful in your life, read *The Parable of the Road*. It's the trip of a lifetime!"

—Chris Baker, author of *The Invitation: How Open and Relational Theology Enhances N.T. Wright's Use of Vocation in Atonement*

"In *The Parable of the Road*, what religious culture so often splits apart—doubt and faith, laughter and lament, intellect and emotion—gets to ride together in the same car."

—Jonathan J. Foster, author of *indigo: the color of grief* and other books

"Please do not call or email to check on the status of a review. We cannot and do not supply information about whether or when a book will be reviewed."   —Publishers Weekly

The Parable of the Road

A NOVEL

by
Brandon Evans

Hardcover: 978-1-968136-22-2
Paperback: 978-1-968136-20-8
Ebook: 978-1-968136-21-5

Printed in the United States of America

Library of Congress Cataloguing-in-Publication Data
The Parable of the Road / Brandon Evans

Prologue

I t was September of 2000. Here's a glimpse into what was going on back then.

ACROSS THE UNIVERSE

The universe containing 100 billion trillion stars spanning 93 billion light-years is expanding at 163,000 miles per hour. Light from a white dwarf that exploded 11 billion years ago finally reaches the Milky Way Galaxy, while a black hole swallows an entire solar system in the distant regions of space.

The events on the third planet orbiting one of the incomprehensible number of burning gas balls hurtling through the void are utterly meaningless when you think about them from this perspective.

But this story is not about the expanding universe.

AROUND THE GLOBE

Technically, in Ethiopia, it's 1992. In Afghanistan, it's 1421. North Korea hasn't even reached the end of the first century. But the countries using the Gregorian calendar are living in a nice round number, so we'll stick with that.

It's a relatively peaceful time on Earth in the late summer of 2000. Representatives from the world's countries are battling over who is the best at running, jumping, and swimming at the Summer Olympics in Sydney, rather than over who has the best god, government, or race.

So the approximately six billion humans alive at the time (aside from the ones with rogue calendars) are beginning a new millennium with the belief that humanity will finally pull it together. This was adorably naive, of course, but remember that the internet was relatively new in 2000 so there was still hope.

IN THE UNITED STATES

A cardboard cutout named Al Gore and a morning drinker called W. are in the middle of the blandest political duel in world history, exchanging scripted smiles during forgettable debates while dodging any controversial policy opinions.

They will eventually take turns declaring themselves to be the new president because, as it turns out, properly marking the candidate of choice on a paper ballot is too complicated for the average rum-drunk Floridian golfer. This is why democracy only works in theory.

The Supreme Court will eventually decide to halt that re-count, enabling W. to win the state of Florida by 537 votes, a mere difference of 0.009%. Don't make me refresh you on the vastness of the expanding universe for you to appreciate how minuscule this margin of victory was.

Despite losing the national popular vote, W.'s win in Florida gives him a 271-266 edge in the electoral college, a constitutional feature invented by men in wigs whose primary concern was saving themselves in taxes, which, as it relates to the 2000 election, is the same motive behind voters who propelled W. to win despite losing.

But the presidential race and its controversial ending are irrelevant to the events chronicled in this story. And the fact that William J. Clinton, or "Billy Boy" as his interns playfully called him, was the sitting president in 2000 matters as little to this narrative as it did back then. So this is the last time U.S. politics will be discussed. Or any global events, since the individuals in our tale are not concerned with what is happening in other countries. Just as the men in wigs dreamed.

SAN FRANCISCO, CA. 710 ASHBURY ST.
ON THE FIRST FLOOR. IN THE BEDROOM.

Casey King traces her finger along the packing tape stretched across the top of a moving box as the bay breeze wafts through her open window. While she stares at the box, she is not thinking about the vast array of galaxies, the other six billion people in existence, or the historic election. Her mind is fixated entirely on the box because it signifies that her life, as she previously knew it, is over.

The point I want to open with as we begin our story is that we are often oblivious to the endless expanse of time and space and people and events beyond our immediate view. Not because we're self-absorbed animals incapable of mindfulness beyond our basic instincts, but because there's enough to try and make sense of in our *own* little universes, the ones inside of us.

But then sometimes, as you'll read, a lucky individual like Casey awakens to the realization that there's far more going on than they previously thought. Not in the distant regions of space, or to foreigners on the other side of our spinning globe, but in their own life. And then they, despite remaining the same size, begin to grow.

Ok, I guess this story is about the expanding universe after all.

Chapter 1

Casey King lifts her eyes from the word "Memorabilia" scrawled in loose cursive across the top of the brown moving box and hollers these words through her open bedroom door: "It's finally the time!"

Her brother Dom, who's lying on a green suede sofa in the living room and rolling a guitar pick between his fingers, gives the appropriate response to her exclamation: "Um, what?"

Casey storms out of her bedroom and marches up to Dom as he casually flicks the pick in the air like a quarter. She looms over him and clarifies her cryptic statement: "It's finally the time to deal with our *father.*"

Dom drops the pick on the rug beneath the couch, nervously adjusts his sweat-stained DC hat, and, still in a horizontal position, clarifies his confused reaction: "Um, *what?*"

Casey ignores Dom's question. She leans over him, straightens a framed poster of the Grateful Dead on the wall, then scoops up crumbs on the armrest under Dom's face, instructs him not to eat on the couch anymore, and strides quickly toward the kitchen.

Dom, slug-like in appearance but with his mind working overtime, still has no idea what she means. This is not the first time his sister has confused him in his lifetime, or today for that matter, but this cryptic statement from Casey has been an extra scramble to his mental eggs. "And by deal with Dad, you mean what exactly?" he asks.

From the kitchen, Casey responds with a matter-of-fact tone, as if it's obvious. "I mean drive to Virginia, march up to him, pull out his Navy Cross, and with that stupid medal in my hand, say 'You want to abandon me? Well, I never needed you in the first place. Here's your fucking Cross back. Fuck you.' Then I'll slam it down, turn around, leave, and never even think about him again." She smiles with satisfaction at the idea.

Dom listens intently to his sister's words, spends a moment pondering them, and replies, "Are you on drugs?" It's the only option that makes sense to him.

"Not at the moment," she huffs. She picks up Dom's cereal bowl from the counter, dumps the milk in the sink, loads it in the dishwasher, and then grabs a pair of scissors from the knife block next to the fridge.

"You think this is going to change anything he's done?" Dom asks.

"Of course not," she says with the scissors firmly in her right hand. "But it's going to make me feel better."

Dom reaches down to the floor to grab the guitar pick, which is just out of reach. He struggles for a moment before giving up, then resumes relaxing on the couch. "Is it, though?"

"Yes, Dom, it is. It will be therapeutic."

"Maybe you should get *actual* therapy, or start a journal, or burn an effigy on Baker Beach, or something else. You don't need to drive across the country to make a point."

"Yes, Dom. I do. My mind is settled. We're going to Virginia."

"*We?*" Dom sits up abruptly. This is not the first time Casey has made plans for him in his lifetime, or today for that matter.

"Yes. We." She grips the scissors and walks briskly toward her bedroom.

"Why am I getting roped into this?"

Casey pops her head out from around the bedroom door-frame. "Because he messed up your life, too. Admit it. Also, I want you there to witness it. Also, you don't have a job, so you have no excuse not to go."

Dom tries to think up a reason why he is unable to join his sister on a cross-country quest for revenge, or, more accurately, to make a dramatic scene, but she's right. He doesn't have a solid excuse.

"It's a straight shot to Arlington from here," Casey says. "Basically I-80 the whole way."

Dom lifts his hat and runs his fingers through his thinning, matted brown hair. "I think your recent stresses have broken the part of your brain that handles reality. You don't need to do this."

Casey stomps back out of her bedroom, once again looms over Dom with her arms folded, scissors still in hand, and proceeds to lecture him. "First off, I don't like your tone. Second, this trip needs to happen, and now is the perfect time. You're unemployed, I'm starting over, so we can finally drive to Virginia and deal with our father."

As the pacifistic offspring of a decorated Vietnam veteran, Admiral Paul King, Dom does not possess the urge to traverse the United States on a retaliation odyssey like his sister does. But as he looks at Casey in her piercing, determined eyes, he is once again reminded that she is the one who inherited whatever gene controls militancy.

"You really think this is going to help you?" Dom asks.

"Yes," she says without hesitation.

"Okay then," he responds. "Let's do it."

"Great," Casey says like she just closed a sale. "I'm going to start packing."

Dom rubs the back of his neck as she returns to her bedroom. "She's finally snapped," he mumbles under his breath as he leans back onto the couch.

Casey doesn't hear him, and wouldn't respond if she had.

CASEY'S BEDROOM. 4:00 PM.

In her bedroom, Casey peers at the final unopened moving box, the cardboard tomb of her past labeled "Memorabilia". It has been sitting undisturbed for six months. She sighs, pushes through the nagging agony inside her, and runs the sharp edge of the scissors across the tape, slicing it cleanly with one smooth motion. She rips open the flaps and looks at the contents inside. Then her stomach drops.

"Dom!" she shouts like she's just witnessed a robbery. "Come here!"

"What is it?" he hollers back.

"Come here. *Now.*"

Dom slowly gets off the couch and sidles into the bedroom, bracing himself for the wrath of Casey. Over what? Unclear. But he knows it's imminent.

"Where is the Cross?" she asks, panicked. "I can't find it. It should be in this box."

Casey aggressively pulls out a string of personal artifacts: a framed 1987 article in the Dallas Morning News with the headline "Local 12-Year Old Wins Software Contest"; her Stanford diploma; a gold medal from the 200-yard individual Medley at the 1993 Texas Swim and Dive Regionals. All cherished mementos, meticulously wrapped in bubble tape. But she tosses them on her bed haphazardly because they are not the one thing in the expanding universe she cares about at that moment.

"I'm sure it's somewhere in here," Dom says with naive optimism.

"No," she snaps back. "The Cross is supposed to be in this box."

Dom can hear Casey's pulse from across the room. He arches one eyebrow as he thinks. "I don't remember seeing it when we moved your stuff," he says. His eyes squint as he tries to recall the details of helping his sister pack her belongings. No luck. His eyes and eyebrows return to their resting position, his focused thinking done for the day. "It's kinda small, you know, so maybe it's wedged between a couple of the other things?"

Casey shakes her head in disagreement. "Impossible," she says. "I keep it safe in a wooden box about this big." She mimes a rectangle in front of her, the dimensions roughly half the width of her chest. "I remember putting it on the dresser next to—"

"Oh shoot," Dom interrupts. Now he remembers. He wishes he didn't.

"What?" Casey responds.

"Shoooooot."

"*What?*" Casey repeats, sternly.

"The little cigar box thing? With the frilly design and silver lock?"

"Yeah!" Casey says excitedly. "It's technically not a cigar box, though; it's a keepsake box. I got it a couple of years ago in Idaho. It's rosewood with custom engravings, but yes, that's it!"

"I know where it is," Dom says, turning his head to the side like he's avoiding eye contact with Medusa.

Casey looks at her brother expectantly, ready for him to reveal the Cross's location within the house.

"It's not in the house," he informs her.

"WHAT?!"

"Shoot," Dom says, still averting his eyes as he prepares to deliver the uncomfortable news.

"Where is it, Dom?"

"It's, um..."

"WHERE IS IT, DOMINIC?"

"It's still with Angie."

"Shit," Casey sighs, sliding her hand down her face, her shoulders slumping. She exhales dramatically as she compulsively adjusts her tight bun. "Why is it with *her*?" She pulls out her Nokia cell phone and begins punching the keypad with shaky fingers.

"It was sitting next to some pictures, and Angie said the items on the dresser were hers. So I didn't think twice about it and left the cigar box. There was a lot of other stuff to pack."

"Dom, it's not a cigar box. Have you ever seen me smoke a fucking cigar? But more importantly, how could you leave it there?" Casey presses the call button aggressively and puts her phone up to her ear.

"Yeah, but, to reiterate what I just said, Angie told me the items in that general vicinity were hers. So I—"

Casey raises her index finger to keep him hushed. *Hey, this is Angie. Leave a message. Beep.*

"Dammit," she mutters as she hangs up. "Voicemail again."

"You don't want to leave a message?"

"No."

A few minutes pass as Casey tensely awaits a return call. Dom doesn't know how to backtrack from what he did, so he physically backtracks towards the kitchen.

Casey glares at her phone. Nothing. Dom returns to the bedroom with a leftover burrito from the night before, smacking his lips with each bite. Casey's index finger rises sharply to her mouth. Dom quiets his chewing. Still nothing from Angie. Dom resumes smacking his lips while munching on the over-stuffed burrito. Casey exhales sharply through her nostrils like a Pamplonian bull. Dom, like a Pamplonian citizen, turns to flee.

"Pack your bag, Dom," Casey commands as he makes his escape. "We're leaving in the morning. And we're making a little detour to Seattle first."

Chapter 2

A few months before that enigmatic exchange between Casey and Dom, the Human Genome Project completed the first-ever mapping of the human genetic blueprint. It was a monumental historical achievement that moved mankind one step closer to understanding who we are. According to genetics, Casey and Dom share more in common with each other than they do with any of the billions of other *Homo sapiens* on Earth. By every other metric, however, they are completely different species.

Ever since they were children, Casey has been the assertive driver of their sibling relationship. Among the earliest and most innocuous examples, then six-year-old Casey convinced then four-year-old Dom to let her cut his hair despite his insistence that "Daddy will be so mad". Casey assured him that their father wouldn't even notice, and proceeded to cut Dom's bangs shorter than those of Julius Caesar. This was not the customary style for suburban Texas kids in the early 80s, or for anyone since the decline and fall of the Roman Empire. The unsanctioned haircut occurred on the eve of Family Picture Day, which was a major problem in this household governed by a strong patriarch who prided himself on order. Contrary to what Casey asserted, their father noticed. And, just as Dom predicted, Daddy was pissed.

So, with over two decades of sisterly pressure behind her, it was a guarantee that Casey would convince Dom to join her on a spontaneous 3000-mile drive from San Francisco, California, to Arlington, Virginia so she could confront their authoritarian father, a man they hadn't seen or talked to in three years. And tacking on an 800-mile detour to Seattle to pick up their father's war medal so it could be used as a prop for Casey's dramatic confrontation didn't dissuade Dom. Casey knew it wouldn't.

AT THE CHEVRON ON THE CORNER OF CASTRO AND MARKET. 7:40 AM.

"Regular is a dollar eighty-six!" Casey exclaims. "Good god. At least this will be the most expensive gas on the trip."

She presses the 87 button. It doesn't register at first, so she repeatedly punches it with the pad of her hand until it does.

Dom sits in the passenger seat, looking at an unfolded U.S. map. His lack of basic U.S. geographical knowledge makes this a discovery-filled read, including his newfound awareness that there is both a North *and* South Dakota. "Oooh, we could go up the coast and see the Redwoods on the way," he suggests through his rolled-down window, having just realized he's lived within a few hours' drive of them for the last five years.

"Why would we do that?" Casey retorts as she shakes the nozzle into place in her forest green '94 Jeep Grand Cherokee. The gas starts pumping.

"Because they're, um, majestic natural wonders and are, you know, on the way?"

"They're *out* of the way," Casey argues. She leans over him, slams her index finger on the map over San Francisco, then traces it up the page. "The fastest route is to go through Berkeley, hit the 505 in Vacaville, and then head up the Five from there. It's a straight shot. I mean, a straight shot in the opposite direction of Virginia, a direction we shouldn't have to go, yet here we are because you left the goddamn Cross behind."

"Does it help to dwell on the past?"

"It helps because it proves that you screwed this one up," Casey volleys back. She stares at the fuel nozzle as if she could intimidate the gas into speeding up. Like the stone-cold fossil fuel that it is, the gasoline is impervious to her pressure and goes at its own pace.

"It would be great to snag some coffee at that Ethiopian place on Castro before we leave town," Dom suggests.

"Naw, grab an energy drink at the convenience store. I just want to get to Seattle."

"But it's right down the street! And we're about to make a twelve-hour drive."

"It's just, shit Dom, it's already a long trip, and it's just been extended a thousand miles. I don't want to add another stop. I just want to get there."

Dom complies and heads into the convenience store while Casey disengages the nozzle from the Jeep and aggressively racks it on the pump. She glances over her shoulder to make sure Dom is out of sight, then reaches into her pocket, pulls out a PEZ dispenser in the form of Homer Simpson, puts it to her mouth, tilts its head back with her thumb, and swallows.

A few minutes later, Dom returns to the Jeep with a Red Bull and a bag of Nacho Cheese Doritos. He hops into the passenger seat, and Casey puts the car in drive before he closes the door. She screeches onto the street and cuts off a VW Bug, then promptly gets flipped off by its gray-bearded driver. She returns the gesture and presses her palm on the horn with enough force to break someone's ribcage. Dom resumes studying the map and learns that there are also two Carolinas.

ON THE BAY BRIDGE. 8:00 AM.

The San Francisco skyline is partially eclipsed by the morning fog as Casey merges onto the Bay Bridge heading east toward Berkeley. Dom looks beyond the suspension cables and onto the white-capped waves below as Casey presses her foot on the gas. She tightly weaves around a truck.

"Ready for some tunes?" Dom asks. Until this moment, the only music that had been playing was Casey's ballad of honking and cussing out slow Bay Area commuters.

"Sure."

"How about some Dave?" Dom suggests, pulling out a

bootlegged copy of Dave Matthews Band *Live at Red Rocks* from a leather CD case.

"No. Something else," Casey snaps. She weaves around a Buick.

"But Dave jams!"

"Dom, Dave Matthews songs are twenty minutes of hell featuring a saxophonist, a dozen cats getting puréed alive, and a yodeler screaming at the top of his lungs. I'm not a frat guy named Kenny in an Abercrombie polo who likes that shit. Absolutely not."

Dom returns Dave to the CD case and turns on the radio. Janet Jackson's "Doesn't Really Matter" is midway through, and Dom starts moving his body to the rhythm, but he wishes Janet used an acoustic guitar like Dave Matthews, sounded like him, and played his songs too.

"Janet cool with you?" he asks.

"Fine," Casey says. She's more focused on how she can wedge the Jeep between an Audi A4 and a semi-truck. She abruptly changes lanes and speeds up to make a pass. Dom reaches to take hold of the grab handle and wonders if Janet will be providing the soundtrack to his death, or if it will be the next song.

When they reach Berkeley, Boyz II Men's "I'll Make Love to You" comes on, and Casey tells Dom to "turn the goddamn radio off".

PASSING FAIRFIELD, CA. 9:00 AM.

The siblings cruise past rolling golden hills veiled in fog. As traffic thins beyond the Bay Area, Casey relaxes just enough for her sisterly guilt to surface. She looks over at Dom, the little brother she's been steamrolling since he was in diapers. He's gazing out the window, whistling "Ants Marching" to himself.

"I know it's a long drive, but at least you'll get to see the countryside along the way," Casey says like she's offering a consolation prize.

"You mean Fairfield?"

"This is not a vacation, Dom. It's a mission."

"Can't it be both?"

"No."

OUTSIDE RED BLUFF, CA. 11:00 AM.

Dom licks his index finger and tries to collect the remaining microscopic Nacho Cheese dust from his empty chip bag. His stomach rumbles. "Can we stop for some food soon?" he asks as they zoom alongside Central California farmland.

"Later," Casey says. "We're making good time."

Dom nods in acknowledgment, looks out his window at the snow-capped Mt. Lassen rising in the distance, and mutters, "You sound like Dad."

"Dom, if you ever say that to me again, I will sever your balls and make you watch me run them over with this Jeep."

APPROACHING YREKA, CA. 12:30 PM.

"Can we stop to eat *now*?" Dom urges.

"Ugh. Fine," she grunts. "It's time to get gas anyway. There are a few fast food spots and a Shell station at the next exit."

"Oh sick. I love that Shell Station. I think I'm feeling some Taco Bell, or maybe Mickey D's. Maybe both."

"Pick one. And whatever you choose, make it quick."

Casey puts PEZ Homer to her mouth as discreetly as she can, pulls his head back, and swallows.

"Can I have one of those in the meantime?"

"No. Get your own."

AFTER LUNCH, JUST ACROSS THE OREGON BORDER. 1:30 PM.

After hastily gobbling half a dozen Soft Taco Supremes, Dom has assumed driving responsibilities for the first time. He hums along to "Otherside" by the Red Hot Chili Peppers playing on the radio. Casey's knuckles are still white even though she hasn't had her hands on the steering wheel for twenty minutes.

"Dom, if you're going to go fifty-five through this whole state, I'm going to lose my shit."

He looks at the speedometer for the first time in twenty minutes and accelerates to 65. Casey stares at the MPH until Dom ups it to 70, and then she looks out at the window at an endless gray sky.

SOMEWHERE SOUTH OF ROSEBURG, OR. 2:30 PM.

Towering Douglas Firs line the interstate while brooding clouds hang above. As the siblings head north on I-5, they pass a billboard for a sex shop, then one for a gun store, and one for a grosser sex shop. Then they pass one with a bright image of a mysterious robed figure with a well-manicured caucasian hand. The words "Jesus is coming for you" span the billboard in block text.

"Did you see that sign? Jesus is coming for you, Dom," Casey snides. "Be prepared."

Dom chuckles uncomfortably, preparing himself to receive a rant. Casey rarely misses an opportunity to pounce on Christian platitudes. She doesn't miss this one.

"Remember, kids," Casey says in a mock-deep voice, emulating their dad. "Believe in Jesus or you will spend eternity grinding your teeth to the gums and wailing for mercy which never comes, ever, because you have rejected your savior and are therefore damned to suffer in eternal conscious torment for your sins against a righteous God. Praise be he!"

"I don't think Dad used to say it like that," Dom responds in hopes she'll shift her commentary to the prevalence of adult shops in conservative rural Oregon. She doesn't.

"Bullshit. It was always 'God's holiness' this and 'the bloody death' that. Every song I knew before I hit puberty was about child sacrifice. Don't you feel like our young minds were corrupted with images of a naked man getting publicly executed?"

"He was wearing a loincloth," Dom says with a smirk.

Casey is not amused and keeps ranting. "When I was eight, I had a nightmare of Satan sticking his tongue in my ear, then roasting me on a spit because my prayers for salvation didn't contain the right words."

"Christ,' Dom utters, disturbed.

"Yeah, exactly. Because I didn't say 'Christ'. I woke up and begged Jesus *Christ* to save me. Eight years old, pleading for my soul and hoping not to lose it on a technicality. You're not still haunted by this shit?"

"I've just chosen to have another perspective on it all."

Casey scoffs. "Well then, enlighten me, oh wise one."

"I just accept that we were raised that way, and it's shaped me into who I am today. It's nobody's fault. I'm just choosing to move beyond the beliefs and chart my own path."

"That is so dumb. It's absolutely somebody's fault."

"Whose?"

"*Whose?*!" Casey throws her hands in the air, her right knuckles smacking the passenger-side window hard enough to bruise. She's unfazed. "God. Men who abuse religious power. Dad. Ignorant sheeple. All culpable. You're so naive, Dom."

Sensing that his sister is not going to dismount from her seething soapbox if he keeps engaging, Dom decides to let the conversation end there. In silence, they drive past a billboard for a sex shop, then one for a gun store, then one for the grossest sex shop.

PASSING THROUGH SALEM, OR. 4:15 PM.

"Can we listen to some Dave now?" Dom asks sheepishly.

"Goddammit. For the last time, no," Casey grunts. "Dave Matthews sucks. End of story."

IN PORTLAND. STALLED UNDER THE BURNSIDE BRIDGE. 5:00 PM.

The Jeep idles in congestion. Inches in front of them is a lime green VW Bug covered in Gore 2000 bumper stickers and sputtering exhaust. Inches behind them is a lifted F-150 with antlers on the hood and a bearded driver wearing a trucker hat with an American flag logo.

"Ugh, if we had left San Francisco earlier, we wouldn't have hit rush hour," Casey laments.

"Eh, I don't think it's helpful to try to rewrite the past," Dom says. "It just is."

Casey nods her head. "Don't you remember the billboard, Dom? Jesus is coming for you. Stop being such a turd."

NEAR OLYMPIA, WA. 7:15 PM.

The gas light comes on, and despite Casey's assertion that they could make it to Seattle, Dom urges her to stop. She acquiesces, then informs him that it's only because she has to pee; that her trusty Jeep has "a sizable reserve tank" and could make it "deep into Canada" if they wanted. Dom decides not to argue this one. It's going to be a long trip, and he needs to save his bullets.

At the 76 station, Dom fills the tank and rehearses something while Casey uses the restroom. She returns to the driver's seat as he re-racks the nozzle.

"Alright, let's go," she says.

"So I, uh, before we take off, I need to ask you something," says Dom nervously as he crawls into the passenger side and clicks his seatbelt on. He's been debating when to raise this question the entire drive. "Does Angie know we're coming?"

"No."

"When was the last time you even talked with her?"

"I mean, we've chatted here and there. We needed to tie up some loose ends and get my name off the lease. So we had a whole conversation about that. And, um, I just think Microsoft has been keeping her busy, so she's been hard to connect with. But in the end, we'll be fine. It just got kind of messy after I moved. But it's not over between us." Casey says this confidently, as if that would make her assertion true.

Dom decides to ask another risky question. "Are we driving all the way to Seattle so you can see her?"

Casey is silent, like she's in an interrogation room and her only out is to plead the fifth.

"It seems like it only makes sense that we're driving to Seattle so you can see her," Dom says. "You could have just texted and asked her to mail the Cross to you."

"Dom, it's just that it's been hard going from being with each other every day for years and then, just like that, nothing. I just feel like we have more to talk about, and the distance is making it hard."

"But what if she threw the Cross away?"

Casey slugs him in the shoulder. "Why would you even suggest that? No way she would do that. Not Angie. What is wrong with you, Dom?"

She puts the Jeep in drive and they screech onto the I-5 on-ramp. Dom rubs his deltoid and realizes he should have peed, too, but he doesn't dare say anything.

Chapter 3

If God and other deities were to hold a draft for young pros-
elytes, Casey King would have been the first person off the
board. When she was five, she starred as Mary in Hollowsprings
Church's Christmas Pageant and took her role so seriously that
she was convinced an angel had *actually* visited her in a dream
to tell her she was going to give birth to the savior of the world.
(Dom was cast as the back hump of a camel, a role he shared
with another boy who also couldn't be trusted to deliver lines
without crying.)

During Sunday school, Casey's teachers would frequently
tell her to let the other kids answer the Bible trivia questions because "God likes it when we share". She absorbed every word her
church/father/evangelical culture taught her about Christianity
and readily accepted simple answers to her queries, like when

she asked her dad, "If aliens exist, do they believe in Jesus too?" The response was an emphatic "Yes." (Admiral King then clarified that extraterrestrials were silly little fictions, unlike biblical inerrancy, a fiery hell, and the rapture.)

So Casey grew up confidently believing that the six-thousand-year-old Earth was created from Monday to Saturday, that a global flood wiped out everyone but the family of a divinely inspired ark builder (and two of every kind of animal, including her favorite, the fox), and that if you said the right prayer in the right way, you'd get to go to heaven. She prayed this prayer a thousand times to make sure she got it correct.

When she was Student of the Week in second grade, Casey listed God as her best friend, as well as Jesus and the Holy Spirit, adding a note at the bottom that the three are the same but different so as to avoid trinitarian heresy.

When she was nine, she memorized the entire book of *Galatians*.

When she was 12, she put on a purity ring and pledged to save herself for marriage.

And when she was 13, she visualized her skin boiling under the intense heat of God's judgment, had a panic attack, and passed out while sitting on the toilet.

CAPITOL HILL, SEATTLE. 8:45 PM.

The Jeep's brakes screech as it comes to a halt in front of a brick apartment building in Capitol Hill. The wipers stop in the middle of the windshield as the engine turns off. Casey takes a deep breath to calm her nerves. It doesn't work. She feels like she's about to get into the pool for an Olympic trial.

"Are you ready for this?" Dom asks, knowing his sister is going to say 'yes' regardless.

"Yes," Casey says with predictable determination. She takes a deep breath to gear herself up for the encounter, but gets distracted by her brother's tightly crossed legs. "What the hell's the matter with you?"

"I have to pee real bad. I haven't gone since lunch."

Dom was never a competitive athlete like Casey was, yet he is exhibiting Olympic-level bladder control. One thought of a splashing pool, however, and he will flood the Jeep.

Casey huffs. "Why didn't you go when we stopped an hour ago?"

"I didn't have the chance!"

"Yes, you did! You had plenty of time! Anyway, not my problem. Hold it. Let's go."

The siblings step out into the misty air and walk up a short flight of wet stairs to a white door illuminated by orange porch lights. Casey rummages in her pocket.

"You still have a key?" Dom asks, perplexed and grabbing himself through his baggy jeans. He wonders if his bladder will sound like a firework when it explodes, or if it will be more like a grenade blast.

"No. Of course not," Casey replies as she removes her hand from her pocket. "Force of habit."

She knocks three times on the door she once used to freely enter. Dom scratches his cheek and bounces around on the stoop to take his mind off his impending urinary detonation. It feels like an eternal wait for both of them.

The door partially opens, and greeting them is a surprised Angie. With her curly hair in a messy bun and a baggy grey Seahawks sweatshirt on, she says the first words Casey has heard her say in months: "Holy shit! What are you doing here?!"

"Hey, Ang," Casey says cooly as if showing up unannounced after an interstate drive is completely normal. "We're in town for something. To see a friend. And other stuff. Things. I tried calling."

"I saw that. You didn't leave a message this time." Angie opens the door some more, but not all the way.

"Right. I figured it would be easier to chat in person."

Angie is clearly not in agreement. She doesn't say a word, so Casey fills in the silence. "What I wanted to ask was, you know that keepsake box of mine that has my dad's war medal in it? The one on our dresser? Could I get that back?"

"Oh yeah," Angie says. "I've been meaning to mail it to you. I can—"

"Angie, I hate to ask this," Dom interjects. "But can I use your bathroom? I'm about to soak my pants."

"Um, sure," Angie responds hesitantly. "Come on in." She steps away from the door to create an opening. Casey casually enters the apartment, and Dom hustles past her. He trots down the hallway, passes by an open bedroom door on the right, glances into it, and then picks up his pace to the next opening. He's in such a hurry that he doesn't shut the door behind him,

CHAPTER 3

29

and Angie and Casey are treated to what sounds like the blast from a firehose hitting a bucket of water.

"You can hang out here," Angie says to Casey as Dom's groan of relief echoes through the living space. "It's in my closet. I'll go grab it."

As Angie walks down the hallway and enters the first door, Casey, standing alone, looks around at an apartment that no longer contains a trace of her previous occupancy. Different couch. Different pictures. Different scent. Casey gasps and blurts out, "She even got rid of our vinyls!?" It's like she stepped into a neighbor's apartment with the exact floor plan she had intimately known for three years. She feels a knot in her stomach twist tighter with each passing second in this strange, familiar place.

Angie returns from the bedroom with the rosewood box and hands it to Casey, who immediately pops open the silver latch. There, secured in the center, is the bronze Navy Cross. Casey gazes at the image of a sailing ship surrounded by a laurel wreath in the middle, a helpful distraction from the pain of being erased. Even though the Cross has been in Casey's possession for years, she doesn't remember the last time she actually laid eyes on it. It's been kept safely in its box and ignored.

"Thank you," is all she can say. Angie nods.

Dom returns from the bathroom, his face no longer grimacing, but he has a startled urgency about him. "We should probably get going, Case," he says. "Thanks, Angie. It was great to see you."

IN THE JEEP. 8:55 PM.

Dom and Casey get back into the Jeep and sit in silence for a few moments. Casey is too preoccupied to notice that Dom hasn't blinked since they left Angie's apartment. After months of separation and confusion, culminating in a twelve-hour drive to finally see Angie in person, the brief, awkwardly transactional exchange was not what Casey expected, let alone was hoping for.

"You okay?" Dom asks.

"Yes," Casey snaps as she turns the key in the ignition. "I'm fine. Let's go find a hotel, I guess."

"Wait, did you think we were going to be invited to stay the night?"

Casey backs out of the parking spot, merges onto the street, and abruptly slams on the gas. When she moved to Seattle three years prior, she felt like she had her whole life ahead of her. Now, returning for the first time since she relocated to San Francisco, she can only see that life through the rearview mirror.

AT THE ADVENTURE MOTEL IN GEORGETOWN, SEATTLE. 11:00 PM.

Casey lies sprawled out on a twin bed with her shoes on while Dom nestles under the covers of his. The motel room smells like a musty ashtray covered with a quick spritz of Lysol. The rumble from a passing train on the tracks next to the motel rattles the door handle. Casey zones out on a dark stain on the ceiling as images of Angie flash in her mind like a funeral slideshow.

"It's like she wants me blotted out of her memory," she laments. "How is this real?"

"Sorry, sis," is all her brother can say, his glazed eyes drooping.

"I don't get it. I've been gone six months. That's it. Six miserable months since I moved. My stuff is still in boxes, and she's already redecorated the entire place? She barely said two words to me. Does she even remember my name? Am I a ghost to her?"

Dom listens while fighting to keep his eyes open. Casey continues to stare at the ceiling and vent her dismay. "I mean, what did I do wrong? She encouraged me to go. 'It'll be good for you,' she said. And then I move, and she tells me she needs space, so I give it to her, and then she tells me it's over. Unbelievable."

Dom has listened to his sister process her breakup for months, meeting her play-by-play and tragic analysis with brotherly compassion.

"I never should have left," Casey moans.

"But you needed to," Dom says with brotherly correction. "To see your vision through."

"No, I didn't. That's the thing," Casey continues. "I could have launched my startup from Seattle. It's not like San Francisco is the only place in the world with the fucking internet. And the result would have been the same. It was a dumb concept anyway. Nobody's ever going to buy groceries online."

"I think that'll happen one day," Dom says.

"What do you know? You have no idea how tech works. You don't even have a cellphone."

"I like the freedom," Dom simply responds. He returns to listening. For months, he has been there as Casey has processed her failed startup, which happened simultaneously with her breakup, so the two traumas often converge into one flowing lamentation.

Casey inhales, then continues venting. "But here I am, the dumbass who thinks that I need to get in the room with venture capitalists, to network with other founders, to get in the scene. Fucking tech bros. Then, of course, crash. Boom. I'm left with nothing, and apparently there are flaming swords blocking me from going back to my old life. Un-fucking-believable."

Casey puts Homer to her lips, tries and fails to swallow, then garbles, "God, my throat is so dry. Is there any water?"

Dom stretches his arm and hands her a plastic Crystal Geyser bottle. She chugs the remainder, then tosses the empty bottle across the room. "Angie was so stiff and cold. I mean, what the hell?"

"Maybe seeing that she's moved on will give you the closure you need to be able to move on, too."

"Wrong. What I need are answers, which I don't get. None of this makes sense. But screw it. Can you turn on the TV? I don't want to listen to myself drone on anymore."

"Sure," Dom says as he reaches for the remote. In the interval between the click of the On button and the picture appearing on the screen, he adds, "Tomorrow's a new day."

"Yeah, but not a better one," Casey grunts.

CNN election commentary plays in the background, but she ignores it and instead fixates on the stain, which, she now surmises, is certainly blood. The splatter pattern makes it obvious. Shit went down here.

When Dom wakes up in the morning, he finds his sister in the same spread-eagled position above the covers. He doesn't ask if she slept; he already knows the answer.

Chapter 4

C asey met Angie on their first day in Palo Alto in the late summer of 1993. They were both freshmen on Stanford's Women's Swimming and Diving team, and, as Casey often tells it, the two made eye contact from across the locker room during the team orientation meeting, and Casey knew deep in her bones that she needed to talk to this person. She approached Angie near her locker and opened the conversation by asking, "So you're new here, too?" The two started talking and never stopped.

In a short time, Casey and Angie learned that they shared a fascination with computers, that they both enjoyed sipping tea on rainy days, both believed cats are superior to dogs, and both had fundamentalist religious upbringings that gave them night terrors, chronic guilt, and dismal pop culture knowledge

(although they did discover that they were both secretly enamored with Boyz II Men.)

They began their relationship fully immersed in each other's lives. As teammates, they trained together, showered together, had classes together, studied together, and ate together. They were, in every way, inseparable. They even convinced their respective roommates to swap living arrangements so they could (unofficially) share a dorm room. For the first time in her life, Casey understood why sappy love songs exist.

She and Angie kept their deepening romantic relationship a secret until graduation night (from their parents, that is. Every teammate, friend, and acquaintance was well aware). Then, over dinner at a Benihana in Mountain View, with hands held tightly, they announced to their mothers and fathers that they had accepted jobs as Software Development Engineers at Microsoft, were moving to Seattle together, and were deeply, madly in love.

The reception of the news by the affluent white evangelical conservatives, as you can imagine, was mixed. While Angie's parents were initially surprised, they realized, in hindsight, that this was a blatantly obvious fact, accepted the news, and grew to embrace them as a couple.

Casey's father, the venerable Admiral King, however, rose from his seat and stormed out of the restaurant. Her mother stood up, hugged Angie, then her daughter, and then followed her husband outside.

Casey chased after Admiral King to explain, but he refused to hear her out. There, in the Benihana parking lot, he lectured her about God's will for sexuality, warned her that she was being deceived, and, when she kept pleading her case, disowned her. He instructed his wife to get in the car and then drove off, leaving his daughter standing there shocked and alone. That was the last time Casey spoke to her father.

So you can see why she might be a little peeved at him.

IN THE ADVENTURE MOTEL PARKING LOT. 7:10 AM.

In the motel parking lot, Dom and Casey walk past yellow caution tape and a lit-up ambulance. Dom unlocks the Jeep and gets in the driver's seat. Casey pulls the water-beaded door handle and is greeted by the keepsake box sitting on the passenger seat. Already a painful reminder of her calloused father, having it returned by an ex-girlfriend now supplies it with the memory of another love gone cold. Casey can't wait to get rid of it. She tosses it in the back, plops down, buckles herself in, and sighs because she's not the one in the ambulance.

ON I-90 EAST OVER LAKE WASHINGTON. 7:30 AM.

"Get around this truck," Casey moans, her eyes half-open.

Dom glances over at her slumped body in the passenger seat. "You rest. We're going fast enough," he says.

"Just get me the hell out of this depressing city of gloom and despair and shattered dreams," she sighs, closing her eyes fully.

Dom waits a few minutes, and, when he believes she's fallen asleep, reaches for the CD case and begins to pull Dave Matthews out. "Don't even fucking think about it," she warns, her eyes still shut. Dave returns to the case.

Dom puts his blinker on and changes lanes. Casey wishes that, when she wakes up, she'll discover this has all been a bad dream. Her life, that is.

APPROACHING CLE ELUM, WA. 9:00 AM.

"Case," Dom says, nudging her shoulder and waking her. "We should get some breakfast."

"Where are we?" Casey mumbles.

"Cle Elum."

"Huh?"

"Cle Elum."

"I heard you the first time. I just don't know what the fuck that is."

"It has a McDonald's. That's what matters. Next exit."

"Eh," Casey responds, half-asleep. "I don't want to stop."

"You need to eat."

"Fine. Hash browns do sound good."

They take the exit and pull into a nearly empty parking lot. Casey grabs the 2000 Rand McNally Road Atlas next to the center console and slams the driver-side door shut on her way out.

They walk into McDonald's, scan the menu, Dom offers to pay, Casey tells him to shove his money up his ass, they order, get their breakfast items, and sit down at a two-person table.

"How are you doing?" Dom asks with concern as Casey slowly nibbles on her hash brown.

"Well my life has disintegrated, my soulmate has gone frigid, and now I'm forcing myself to stuff down a stale potato brick in a podunk town en route to scream at the person who fucked my whole life up. Other than that, I'm just dandy. How are you?"

"I'm good," he says with a full mouth of Egg McMuffin.

"That was a rhetorical question. I know you are. You're the lucky one."

While chewing and nearly chipping a molar on her hash brown, Casey places her finger on the map and traces it along I-90 to Billings. "It's probably a ten-hour drive from here. Assuming I'm driving, of course. We'd hopefully get there by the dawn of the next millennium if you're behind the wheel."

"We can't have this aggressive of a pace the whole way," Dom says. "You don't need to be in such a rush. We're going in the right direction, and we'll get there when we get there. Maybe we can just enjoy the ride?"

"We can enjoy the ride when we're done with this mission. Let's push it to Billings and stay the night there. Hopefully we can find a hotel room that wasn't the scene of some fortunate soul's grizzly death. We'll assess after that. All I need is for it to be smooth sailing from here."

Dom shrugs. "Sounds good to me."

They take their last bites, get up from the table, throw away their trash, exit the McDonald's, and walk to the Jeep. Then Casey discovers that the rear driver's side tire is completely flat.

"Goddammit."

AT LES SCHWAB TIRE CENTER. CLE ELUM, WA. NOON.

As they wait for a new set of tires, which Dom offered to pay for and was immediately reminded by his sister that his money belonged up his ass, Casey sips on watered-down Folger's from a styrofoam cup while Dom flips through the June 1996 issue of *Car and Driver Magazine*. The Service Technician comes up and tells them it'll be another hour. Casey grunts.

"It's a minor inconvenience," Dom says to her.

"Well I'd appreciate a minor *con*venience at some point on this trip."

BACK ON THE ROAD. SOMEWHERE BETWEEN MOSES LAKE AND RITZBURG, WA. 2:30 PM.

Back behind the wheel, and in the middle of farmland with few cars in their vicinity, Casey presses the gas and sets the cruise control at 90. To calm his nerves, Dom reaches into the back, grabs the keepsake box, and opens it. He examines the Cross, which he hasn't seen since he was a kid.

"It is pretty cool," he says. "Shiny."

Casey nods.

"I remember when Dad gave it to you. You were always so proud that he had earned it and would always ask to hold it, so I get why he chose to give it to you. You were always his favorite. How old were you again?"

"Twelve."

"Oh yeah, twelve. That's right. It's a big deal that he passed it on to you."

"I know. He made sure everyone knew. I shouldn't have accepted it."

Dom is caught off guard. This is the first time in thirteen years he has ever heard Casey speak negatively about receiving the Cross. "Why not?"

"Because it's been more of a burden than a blessing," she says. "One fucking heroic feat way before we were born and that's supposed to be at the center of everything. Always talking about it. Bullshit. It doesn't actually mean anything to me. It's just a thing. But to him, it's apparently everything."

"It means he saved a bunch of people's lives. It's a big deal."

"Sure, and good for those poor teenagers who were saved from dying in a pointless war so they could return to the States with missing limbs and heroin addictions. Glad Dad saved them. But he abandoned me. Then he abandoned you and Mom. I'm so ready to slam this dumb hunk of metal down in front of him, drop verbal napalm, and be done with his shit forever."

"I still don't understand why you feel the need to do this."

"Justice, Dom."

"Seems more like vengeance."

"Eh, what's the difference?"

PASSING THROUGH COEUR D'ALENE, ID. 5:00 PM.

They drive by forested hills and a shimmering lake reflecting the late afternoon sun.

"It's beautiful here," Dom says while looking out the passenger window at sailboats floating above the water's surface.

Casey's voice crackles. "Angie and I came to Coeur d'Alene for a weekend once. We rented a cabin in the woods, sailed on the lake, and spent the evenings sipping wine by the fireplace. I got the keepsake box that houses that goddamn Cross at a boutique downtown. It was a magical weekend. All tainted now."

"We should talk about something else," Dom says, hoping to think of a subject that doesn't remind Casey of Angie, or love, or Dad, or the dotcom crash, or life in general.

"Like what?" she says as if she's goading him to take a step and get blown up by a land mine. He can feel it. He can't think of anything safe to discuss, so they sit quietly as the radio plays in the background. Casey's phone starts ringing. She looks down at the lit-up screen in the cup holder of the center console.

"No fucking way!"

"What?"

"Look who's calling."

She holds the phone up. The caller ID displays three letters: M.O.M.

"Do you want me to answer it?" Dom asks.

"Absolutely not!" Casey says sternly. "I don't have the capacity to deal with her, too. She's complicit in all of this."

"I don't think so, Case," Dom says. "She's always been there for us. It would be good for you to talk to her."

"Bullshit. She just stood there while he berated me. Didn't even defend me. Coward. She's as much to blame as he is."

Casey gets a notification that she has a voicemail. She doesn't listen to it.

20 MILES WEST OF MISSOULA, MT. 8:30 PM.

A light rain patters on the windshield as lightning flashes on the horizon of a dark sky. Casey yawns and slaps her cheek with an open palm, frustrated with herself for not being able to stay eternally alert despite having had insomnia for months. Dom watches her with concern from the passenger seat.

"It's getting late. We should stop for the night in Missoula," he suggests. "You look pretty tired."

"No, I don't," Casey responds, avoiding her face in the rear-view mirror. "I look fine."

"If we were flying across the country, you'd have to check the bags under your eyes."

Casey grimaces. "Don't make fun of my appearance, asshole. I don't make fun of you for being bald at twenty-three."

"I'm bald*ing*," Dom clarifies. "And you make fun of me for that all the time."

"I'm fully awake, Dom. I just fired down that Red Bull. I can feel the veins in my forehead throbbing. That's focus juice. Let's make it to Bozeman at least."

"Sleep would probably be better for you."

"I'll sleep when I'm dead, which will hopefully be soon."

Dom adjusts his hat without showing his receding hairline and watches a bolt of lightning illuminate the distance. Dave Matthews remains safely tucked away in the CD case, free from ridicule for the moment.

AT A (SLIGHTLY) NICER MOTEL IN BOZEMAN, MT. 12:30 AM.

Casey puts Homer to her lips, pulls his head back, takes two, then walks away from the bathroom in baggy sweats and a t-shirt, turns off the light, and collapses on her creaky mattress. Dom is already tucked into his bed with his eyes shut. Casey pulls the covers down, slides under them, rolls over, and closes her swollen eyes. She tells her brain to shut off, but the stubborn sponge refuses to.

"This room's not so bad," Dom says in the dark.

"Mhmmm," she responds, nestling into her bed to give her body peace even though an endless war is being waged inside it.

"If you want, I can pay for a better hotel at our next stop," Dom says. "Maybe it'll help you sleep better."

"For the last time, shove your money up your ass. And stop talking. That's what's keeping me awake."

Just when it seems like Casey's nervous system is about to call a ceasefire so she can drift off to sleep, the muffled sound of voices begins to emanate from the room behind their beds, followed by rhythmic thumping, squeaking, bass and treble moaning, and the vibrations of a slamming headboard on the other side of paper-thin drywall.

Dom, barely awake, asks, "What's that noise?"

"Well, either two gorillas are auditioning for WWE or a happy couple is having a great time," Casey laments.

"At least our beds are pretty comfy," Dom says before drifting soundly to sleep.

Casey covers her head with a pillow as she waits for the couple to stop so she can lose consciousness. They don't, so she doesn't.

Chapter 5

If you wanted to pick the worst time in human history to start a web-based company, the beginning of the year 2000, when Casey launched hers, would be it.

Belligerent excitement over the internet's revolutionary potential spurred investors in the late 90s to pour cash into tech startups founded on hype, unsustainable business models, and obnoxious Super Bowl ads starring sock puppets.

One of the most emblematic failures of the era was Flooz. com, which offered a digital currency that could be used to purchase goods from participating online merchants. With flashy marketing campaigns featuring Whoopi Goldberg and the naive assumption that consumers would trade real U.S. dollars for something called a Flooz credit to buy things like pet food and books, tens of millions of dollars were pumped into the company by speculative investors. It was a frenzy.

Then, like every stock market bubble that had burst before it, the pop was loud and sudden, and trillions of dollars in market value were wiped out within a matter of weeks. Seemingly overnight, scores of dotcom founders, including Flooz.com and CityCart, Casey King's company, were forced to file for bankruptcy.

In the aftermath of the dotcom crash, Casey was so distraught that she vowed never to use the internet again. And she even refused to support that shit-licking robot Al Gore (her words) because he ludicrously claimed to have invented it.

AT A ROADSIDE DINER IN BILLINGS, MT. 10:30 AM.

Seated in a booth with syrup stains, Dom studies the map next to his plate of pancakes and bacon. He runs his fingers over the paper Eastern Seaboard, and says, "I wish we could go to New York City since we're going to be on that side of the country. It's pretty close to Virginia."

"It's nowhere near Virginia," Casey refutes. She tilts her chin up and chugs her steaming coffee, then chases it with a bite of her waffle.

"Well, like, relatively speaking it is," Dom responds. "How sick would it be to stay at the Plaza Hotel like Kevin from *Home Alone 2* and get room service and then go to the East Village and jam with some bohemian bros?"

"We're not going to fucking New York City, Dom. End of story."

Dom returns to his careful study of the road atlas and stumbles upon a route peculiarity. "Oh, this is interesting," he says, pointing at the map. "The highway forks near Billings." He hands the open Rand McNally to Casey. She analyzes the divergence of I-90 and I-94 with the same intensity she applied when assembling her first computer at the age of ten. Meanwhile, a waitress who was either born in the late 1800s or is a 32-year-old chain smoker shakily refills their coffee cups and mostly succeeds at it.

"Both routes eventually lead us to Chicago," Dom adds, "which we have to go through anyway, and both are about the same distance." He sits back, pleased with his eyeball-measuring skills.

"Huh," is all Casey says. She peers intently at the map as she takes a bite of her waffle. "You're right."

"I vote we go the northern route," Dom says. "It'll take us through Minneapolis. I've heard that place is rad. Good music scene—Dylan was there, Casey. Dylan! Plus, there are a lot of hot chicks."

Casey soaks up spilled coffee with her napkin. "How do you know there are a lot of hot chicks?"

"I don't know. Midwest city chicks are just hot. They have the glow that comes from years of drinking whole milk, and they strum the strings of my heart with their accents. And Minneapolis is a big city. Math."

"What a dumb generalization."

Dom shrugs and takes a bite of his pancake. Casey motions that he has syrup on his chin. He wipes it with his napkin and ends up with more on his chin. She gives up.

"I think we should go the southern route," she says. "South Dakota is the same flat wasteland as North Dakota, I assume. So that's a wash. But there's no city traffic to slow us down. We can get to Chicago faster if we go south."

"But Midwest city chicks!"

"Chicago is the Midwest too, dipshit. But this is not a hookup tour, Dom. You wouldn't get any chicks anyway. You're an unemployed scrub."

"It'd be worth a shot, though. Ok, here's what I propose: we flip a coin. Heads, we go north through Minneapolis. Tails, we go south through, uh…" He looks at the foreign word on the map. "Si-ow-cks City. Deal?"

Maybe it's because the sugar from the maple syrup has reached the part of Casey's brain that is open to possibilities. Maybe she just wanted to win at something. Regardless, she answers, "It's pronounced *Sue* City. And whatever. Deal."

Dom pulls a quarter out of his pocket along with a couple of candy wrappers and a ball of lint. He extracts the quarter from the trash and places it on his thumb. Fate is in his hands. "So if I win, we can do something fun in Minneapolis, right?"

"Ugh, ok."

"But if you win, can we at least stop at Mt. Rushmore?" he asks.

"No. It's just faces carved on a rock. Absolutely not."

Dom nods, inhales through his nostrils, and flicks the quarter into the air. It flips rapidly as it rises, then succumbs to gravity, lands on his fork, and bounces off the table as the 32/102-year-old waitress passes by carrying a tray of skillets over her shoulder. The quarter rolls to a stop in the middle of the tiled aisle. Dom and Casey look down at it. Heads.

"Figures," Casey grunts.

Dom pumps his fist, then shoves his pancake-loaded fork into his mouth.

Chapter 6

The benefit of growing up in a household led by Admiral King was the predictable, organized life. Three square meals, preceded by prayers, were provided at the same time every day. The children were assigned daily Scripture readings, and there was an extensive chore list with a strict schedule posted in the kitchen. Bedtime, preceded by another prayer, was at 8:30 sharp. And there was weekly Sunday school, followed by Sunday service, followed by lunch at the Kip's Big Boy in Fort Worth. Every Sunday.

Next to the chore list was a chart with the kids' names accompanied by sticker stars earned for accomplishments like A-grades, athletic successes, and general rule adherence. Casey ran out of real estate next to her name, so she placed stars in the empty boxes next to Dom's.

Casey, as you can imagine, thrived in the rigid structure. Dom, and this goes without saying, was quite familiar with the stinging sensation of a wooden spoon slapping his bare, pink ass.

I-94 EAST, APPROACHING THE INVISIBLE LINE DIVIDING MONTANA AND NORTH DAKOTA FARMLAND. 2:30 PM.

Casey grips the steering wheel and looks out at a straight stretch of highway disappearing into the horizon while Dom pulls the bill of his hat over his face and tries to rest.

"Is it raining?" he asks with his eyes shut.

"Nope," Casey answers with annoyance. "Bugs."

The pitter-patter of insects hitting glass intensifies as they pass by a sign reading "Welcome to North Dakota." Casey pulls the wiper control, sprays pale blue washer fluid, and watches the blades smear mosquito guts in arching streaks across the windshield. Dom positions himself, then repositions to the other side, then back, then back again, then starts snoring as soon as he finds his spot. Casey wonders how he is always able to sleep so easily, and concludes that it's because his simple mind doesn't have much to think about. She sprays another round of fluid on the windshield and maxes out the blade speed.

SOMEWHERE FLAT. 4:00 PM.

The wiper blades vigorously oscillate on the windshield/mosquito Gettysburg. The highway is still straight. The mountains are still somewhere else.

Casey has not ceased ruminating on the sinking ship that is her life. And she's hellbent on sailing that ship to Virginia so she can have one last battle with the one who put the hole in it.

"Now would be a good time to plan out the rest of the trip," she says. "Figure out the fastest way to get there. Can you grab the map?"

Dom pulls it out from in between his seat and the center console, opens to the two pages containing the entire United States, searches for what seems like forever to his sister, and eventually places his finger in the middle of North Dakota, where he guesses they are.

"We're obviously going to be driving this way for a long ass time," she says with one eye on the map and the other on the road. "How many miles is it from Bismarck to Minneapolis?"

Dom looks down at the mileage scale at the bottom, sets his index finger and thumb about an inch apart, and incrementally moves them along I-94 to Fargo, then down through St. Cloud, and over to the Twin Cities.

"I don't know, like 400 miles." He starts to double-check his math but quits.

"I'll trust you since I can't do it myself right now. Assuming you don't take another marathon dump, that means we can probably get there around eight or eight thirty. Then we can find a hotel and you can fail to hunt down your mythical Midwest farmer's daughter."

"Not a farmer's daughter. A Midwest *city* chick."

"You men are turds."

"Why are you lumping us all together?"

"Because you're all turds."

"You get feisty with me for generalizing the beautiful Midwest hunnies and then get to categorically trash the entire male population? That's how this works?"

"Yes. You men are all the same. Kevin McIntosh, for example. Tried to finger me after prom. I smacked the shit out of him. Or the drunk college guys who told me that they, too, were breaststroke champions. Or the fucking tech bros. Or Dad. Or you. You're all turds."

"I'm not! I'm just a chill dude hoping to find a nice Minnesotan babe who cooks casseroles and keeps me cozy at night." The mere thought of that future fills Dom's heart with the warm fuzzies, a sensation Casey believes is a fiction created by our bodies to dupe us into spinning around on a meaningless space rock long enough to pass our genes on to another victim.

"You're an absolute turd." Casey pulls the wiper control, but it shoots blanks. "Oh goddammit," she sighs.

"What?"

"We're out of fluid."

Dom does not pick up on the gravity of the situation. He hums along to Creed's "With Arms Wide Open" playing faintly on the crackling radio. Casey repeatedly pulls the wiper control as if it will magically produce fluid. It doesn't.

"All we're doing is smearing bug splatter across the glass. At this rate, my view will be completely blocked by a layer of wings and ooze before this shitty song ends."

"We can just stop at a gas station and get some more," Dom suggests.

Casey dramatically turns her head from side to side. "Do you see a gas station around here, Dom? You think that silo over there in the distance is storing jugs of wiper fluid, you moron?"

"Easy," Dom says like he's trying to tame a wild stallion. "I mean, the next gas station we *can* stop at."

"We won't make it that far," Casey snaps. She pulls the Jeep off the shoulder. "Give me your water bottle."

Despite being thirsty due to inhaling an entire bag of Doritos, Dom hands her his half-finished Crystal Geyser. She snatches it from him, opens her door, hurries out, dumps the water on the windshield, and then hurries back in, slamming the door behind her. "Gross. There are millions of mosquitoes out there."

She smacks her forearm and restarts the wiper blades, which are able to clear enough of a view to satisfy her. She puts the car in drive and screeches back onto the highway so the King siblings and dozens of mosquito hitchhikers can find civilization.

Twenty miles down the road, they take the exit for a lone gas station. Dom fills the tank as Casey marches into the convenience store. The clerk informs her that they're out of wiper fluid. She marches back to the Jeep and tells Dom it's his turn to drive. Then she gets in the passenger seat, puts Homer to her mouth, closes her eyes, and tries to tune out the world at large. But its volume knob is turned to ten and stuck.

I-94 WEST, APPROACHING THE INVISIBLE LINE DIVIDING NORTH DAKOTA AND MONTANA FARMLAND. 6:00 PM.

Casey repositions her body to the right side, then the left, then back to the right. She lets out a groan, then squashes a mosquito on her forearm. She'd relish in the execution if it weren't for the itch. Dom turns Dave Matthews off in anticipation of her waking in order to avoid the same fate as the bloodsucker.

"Great call going this route, dumbass," Casey says with her eyes still shut. "I hate bugs."

Dom, with one hand on the wheel, responds, "There probably would have been mosquitoes in South Dakota, too."

"We'll never know, will we?" she retorts.

"I guess not," he shrugs.

Casey yawns, stretches her arms, and sits upright. She rubs her eyes and looks at the road ahead, which is barely visible through the ever-thickening layer of bug guts smeared on the windshield.

"Wow, this part of the country is something else, huh?" she says while looking through a small opening in the windshield. "It all looks the same."

"Yeah, it's pretty flat. The good news, though, is I've been driving really fast. We're making good time."

"Great," Casey says through a yawn. She looks out the passenger window in time to see a sign reading "Welcome to Montana", and then goes from drowsy to fully alert in one blink.

"Are you fucking kidding me?" she shouts. "Are you *fucking* kidding me?" she repeats, louder.

"What?" Dom says, confused and scared.

"We're going in the wrong direction!" She checks the clock in a panic. "Oh god, we've been going for TWO HOURS in the wrong direction! You brain-dead slug, what in the name of the horrible despot of the universe is fucking wrong with you?!"

"Hmmmm," Dom hums as he peers beyond the insect corpses. "Dang, yeah, I thought this all looked familiar. But it's pretty hard to tell through the windshield. There's lots of bugs on it."

"Pull the goddamn car over!" Casey screams. "I'm driving!"

Dom steers the car off the shoulder and coasts to a stop. Casey throws her door open, strides around the front of the Jeep, shoves Dom as he passes by her, then gets into the driver's seat, slams the door, puts the car in drive, makes a sharp U-turn, and burns rubber pulling onto I-94 East.

"We could probably use this as an opportunity to get some wiper fluid," Dom says as he clicks his seatbelt in. Casey squashes a mosquito on her leg, then punches Dom on the arm.

SOMEWHERE EVEN FLATTER. 9:30 PM.

Lightning strikes in the distance, revealing a level horizon. Despite being on an interstate highway, they haven't seen a car heading in their direction for miles. Only Casey is lonelier than this road.

"You know what would really spice this trip up? A good book on tape," Dom says facetiously as he sifts through a case of his sister's cassette tapes he pulled out from under his seat. They are all beyond his education level. "Perhaps a riveting Gore Vidal work?" Dom has no idea who this is.

"I'm not in the mood, Dom," Casey says, her hands gripping the steering wheel tightly.

"For a good ole narration of the decline and fall of the American empire by the dynamic Gore Vidal?" Dom has no idea what he is saying.

"For your snark, you turd. I'm tired and need to pay attention to the road."

"I, for one, would like to add a little fun to this trip. Explore some cities. Meet some people. Have some adventures. You know, while we're young."

"I'm over the hill," Casey says.

"You're twenty-five."

"Exactly," she says. "There's a whole new wave of twenty two-year-old Ivy grads flooding tech while I'm a washed-up failure destined for an I.T. job in Oakland for the rest of my—OH JESUS WHAT THE FUCK!!!!"

Dom directs his attention to the road just in time to witness a deer's final breath before it collides with the front grille of the '94 Jeep Grand Cherokee.

ON THE SIDE OF I-94. 30 MILES WEST OF FARGO, ND. 10:20 PM.

Dom watches from inside the Jeep as Casey frantically motors around with her cellphone to her ear, periodically looking back at the deer carcass resting in front of the dented hood, then pulling her phone away from her ear to find a signal, and back and forth. At one point, she throws her hands up to the sky in anger at Verizon or God, probably both.

She returns to the car and slams the passenger door as she gets inside. "I finally got enough cell service and called for a tow truck," she informs Dom. She slams her phone in the cupholder of the center console.

The siblings sit in silence. Dom counts the cars that zoom by. One. Casey's phone starts buzzing. She looks down at the display, sees "Mom" on the caller ID, and snorts. "Nope!"

"Come on, give Mom a chance," Dom urges.

"Ugh. No," Casey retorts. "I can't even stand to hear her voice."

"When was the last time you talked to her?"

"I don't know. A while ago. She won't stop calling, though. But I don't care what she has to say."

The call goes to voicemail.

"This is just perfect, Dom," Casey groans. "Stranded in the middle of nowhere because God determined that the coin would land on heads."

"It was just random chance," Dom responds. "If it were tails, maybe we would have hit a moose or something on the other route. This isn't anybody's fault."

"Not according to Dad!" Casey puts on her gruff, imitation father's voice. "Remember, kids, God is sovereign over all things. He causes the blades of grass to grow and knows every hair on our head. There's no rogue atom in the universe! Therefore, God is responsible for all the good things in life, but conveniently can't be blamed for the bad. That's how it all works!"

"I don't think Dad would say it like that," Dom says.

"I mean, that's the basic idea, right? God is in total control! He sent a lamb to Abraham so he could slaughter it, so that means he sent the deer for my bumper to do the same, right? *Right?* Or that one wasn't his doing for some reason?"

"Dad always said that bad things came from sin and the devil."

"Oh, yes. Of course. Like when he told me to thank God for the goldfish I got when I was five, but when I found it floating upside down the next morning, he told me it was because Adam ate naughty fruit and death became a thing. That's ridiculous. Who created the devil? Who set the world up to fail? *God.* That's who. None of it adds up. A dumbass wins the lottery and it's 'praise the Lord!' But a kid in Gaza gets blown up by an IED on the way to school, and it's not God's will. Make it make sense."

"I like to think that a lot of what happens is out of my control, so I just focus on what's in my power."

"Easy for you to say. You're the lucky one. God hates me. He's probably scattering nails across the countryside like a deranged Johnny Appleseed in anticipation of me driving down those roads next."

"I don't think that's true. God doesn't hate you."

"Oh, you don't think so? You're a theologian now, are you? How about Dad thanking God for forming me in the womb to be smart and athletic, but then it's my fault because I was born queer? Bullshit. I hate him so much. I hate everything about him."

"God or Dad?"

"Yes."

"A lot of people have been led to think those things, Case, including Dad." Dom can't believe he's defending his father, but he doesn't want to add fuel to Casey's fire and brimstone. "Like he always said, not that I agree with him, but being a servant of God means trusting his word."

"Well I'm tired of dealing with the servants. I want to speak to their fucking manager."

Headlights from behind illuminate the inside of the Jeep, and the theological sparring ceases. As a dark figure approaches, Dom spins the handle and lowers the driver's side window. A uniformed man with the name Jesús embroidered on his left chest approaches. "Hello," he says in a thick Spanish accent. "You called for a tow?"

Dom turns to his sister. "See, Casey. Jesus did come for us. The billboard was right all along."

AT THE BEST VALUE MOTOR LODGE IN FARGO, ND. 2:00 AM.

Casey hangs up the corded phone on the nightstand between the beds. "The auto body shop's answering machine says it opens at 7:30," she says. "We'll walk over there then."

"Hopefully it's a pretty quick fix," Dom answers. He picks up the TV remote and changes the channel to a rerun of SportsCenter.

"I'm not that lucky," Casey bemoans. "But maybe some of yours will finally rub off on me."

Dom is too enamored by Chris Berman proclaiming "Back back back gone!" over a steroid-fueled Barry Bonds dinger to remind Casey that he, too, is in the same predicament as she is. "The Giants beat the Dodgers," he says matter-of-factly to a woman who has never had a thing for ball sports. "I think this is finally their year."

Casey doesn't respond. She adjusts her pillow, then puts Homer to her lips, lies on her back, and stares at the ceiling. She feels a tickle in her ear. "Oh for the love of God!" she shouts.

She springs out of the bed, rips off the covers, and rushes to the sink. Dom's eyes follow her, but his brain remains focused on the N.L. West Division race. Casey returns to the bed and slams the opening of a plastic cup onto the sheets. "I got the little fucker!" she exclaims. She scoops the cup off the bed, flips it right side up, covers it with her hand, and bolts out of the room.

Dom resumes watching baseball highlights. "Eh, actually it's probably going to be the Yankees again," he says out loud despite being the only person there.

Casey charges through the parking lot, parts two cigarette-smoking youths like they're the Red Sea, flings open the door to the motel's front desk, stampedes toward the concierge, and slams the cup onto the counter. "Do you see this? Do you *see* this?! There are fucking bed bugs in my fucking room."

"Aw not again," a moustached nightshifter named Jim whines.

STILL AT THE BEST VALUE MOTOR LODGE IN FARGO, ND. 3:00 AM.

In a different room, which Jim swore had been fumigated recently, "Honest to God," he said, Casey furiously scratches an itch, loses consciousness, then awakens, scratches another itch, then loses consciousness, on repeat.

Dom is sound asleep and snoring loudly.

AT AL'S AUTO IN FARGO, ND. 9:30 AM.

While waiting for the Jeep's diagnosis, Casey sips on watered-down Folger's from a styrofoam cup while Dom flips through the July 1996 issue of *Car and Driver Magazine*. The Service Technician comes up and tells them that it'll be another hour. Casey grunts.

"I'm not dealing with another shitty motel," she says. "My old swimmate Vanessa lives in Chicago. I'm going to call and see if we can crash with her for the night." Casey leaves the waiting room. Dom flips the page and goes, "Wow."

A few minutes later, Casey returns with a smile. "We're all good. Got us a place to stay."

"Sweet," Dom says to both Casey's announcement and the picture of the new (for people in 1996) BMW M3 on the page in front of him.

Casey plops down on a metal folding chair and lets her mind wander. She thinks about a time she and Angie placed first and second at the Stanford Invitational, then cuddled on the floor of their apartment, drinking white wine and laughing. The warm memory of being weightlessly in love is overridden by the sharp sting of loss, giving way to surging anger as she flashes back to the phone call with Angie, where she was told, bluntly, that their relationship was over. Seven years together, ending in a long-distance call. Casey sighs. Then an intrusive image of her dad whipping Dom with his belt flashes into her mind. Casey grits her teeth. The snowballing mental horror film is thankfully interrupted by a service technician.

"Good news," the portly man with thick stubble and a grease-stained uniform says. "There wasn't any significant damage."

"See," Dom says, looking up from his magazine and over at his sister. "We got lucky."

"That is, aside from significant cosmetic damage, obviously," the technician continues. "The hood, grille, and front bumper all need to be replaced."

"How long will that take?" Casey asks.

"I don't know, one or two."

"Hours?"

"No. Weeks. We don't have '94 Jeep hoods lying around here, ma'am. We need to order parts."

"Screw that. I can live with a dented car. Let's go, Dom."

ON I-94 PASSING THROUGH THE NORTHWEST SUBURBS OF MINNEAPOLIS. 1:30 PM.

The check engine light is on, but Casey doesn't care. Dom gazes out at the downtown skyline of the City of Lakes in the distance. His dream girl is somewhere out there, meeting another man she'll spend her life with, eating casserole, and snuggling under furry blankets on cold winter nights.

"Minneapolis is lovely," he says longingly.

"Shut up, Dom."

Chapter 7

The problem with being a successful, ambitious person is that you tend to associate with other successful, ambitious people.

Since Casey was a child, her fierce drive alienated her from other competitive girls, resulting in a brutal inner conflict between personal achievement and human connection. When she was in middle school, for example, Casey was excluded from Brittany Beck's birthday sleepover because she dominated her in a pickup basketball game during P.E. Casey spent the night alone in her bedroom wondering if she should sandbag it during her next competition for the sake of being popular, then concluded that, no, she was just going to kick everyone's asses even more.

Despite the social damage it caused, Admiral King encouraged Casey to keep striving for excellence, assuring her that it was God's will for her to work diligently as a faithful Christian soldier. Quoting the book of Colossians, he exhorted her:

"Whatever you do, do it heartily, as to the Lord and not to men, knowing that from the Lord you will receive the reward of the inheritance; for you serve the Lord Christ." Then, turning to Dom, he finished the passage: "But he who does wrong will be repaid for what he has done, and there is no partiality." Casey nodded in agreement. Dom hung his head.

Casey's determination eventually led her beyond the drama of teenage relationships, earned her a scholarship to Stanford, and released her from her suburban Texas prison. Surrounded by collegiate peers who respected her intelligence and ambition, and removed from her authoritarian religious context, she was able to discover, surprisingly, who she really is. And when she was with Angie, Casey felt like she could truly be herself for the first time in her life.

She made the occasional visit back to the place of her up-bringing on summer breaks and holidays, but it no longer felt like home.

LINCOLN PARK, CHICAGO, IL. 7:30 PM.

The dented Jeep's brakes screech as it comes to a halt in front of a row of brick townhomes. The siblings slowly emerge from the vehicle. Dom grabs their bags from the back while Casey stretches her hamstrings, and they walk toward townhome num-ber one.

"It's rad that Vanessa is letting us stay with her," Dom says with a duffel bag strap in each hand. "This neighborhood is legit."

"Yeah, I can't wait to sleep on a mattress that doesn't stab me with rusty coils," Casey responds.

When they reach the front door, Casey taps a brushed nickel knocker three times while Dom leans against a decorative railing under hanging pots of flowers. The door opens. Greeting them is bubbly, pristine-faced Vanessa.

"Holy shiiiiiiit! What are you doing here?!" Vanessa squeals. She gives Casey a giant embrace and bounces up and down. "Oh my god, I can't believe you're actually in Chicago. Hey Dom!"

"Hey Vanessa," he says. "It's been a while."

"I know, right?!" Vanessa giggles. "Come on inside."

They enter the townhome, which has wood floors, crown molding, and an interior that must have been decorated by a British debutante named Beatrice who had a flair for ornate chandeliers and throw pillows with golden tassels. Casey would be jealous if she weren't so happy to be sleeping in a place that doesn't smell like Camel Lights. Dom asks where the bathroom is, and Vanessa points him down a long hallway. She's still smiling like her cheeks are permanently stuck in that position.

Casey surveys Vanessa's Windy City palace. "This place is… majestic. How many bedrooms are there?"

"Six!" Vanessa responds enthusiastically.

"Wow. And you live here by yourself?"

"Oh no, of course not. My wonderful fiancé, Kensington, lives here too. He's in London on business. His family is in league with the Crown, you know."

"Oh, yeah, Kenny. Haven't seen him since he was puking in the bushes on grad night. Well congratulations. I didn't know you got engaged."

"This summer, actually!" Vanessa beams. She waves her left hand and flashes a monstrous, shining ring that nearly blinds Casey. "Kensington surprised me over dinner at the Bellemore in the West Loop, then surprised me even more with a fabulous gala on the rooftop. Madonna performed for us. It was utterly divine."

"You are pretty networked, huh?"

"Well, I am the daughter of a Senator," Vanessa says.

"Mmmm. I, too, am the daughter of an asshole," Casey replies under her breath.

"Huh?"

"Nothing."

Dom returns from the bathroom, and Vanessa shows the siblings their elaborately decorated guest rooms, complete with plush bedding and framed pictures of the English countryside. Dom soars onto his bed like a flying squirrel.

"So what's new with you?" Vanessa asks Casey as she sets her bag down on a cherry wood credenza.

"You know, nothing much. Still in San Francisco, putting the pieces of my life together and figuring out what's next."

Vanessa places her hand on her heart. "Oh, honey," she says. "I was so sorry to hear about your startup. Angie told me."

"Wait, you talked to her? What's she been up-"

Dom bursts out of the spare room of his dreams and into the spare room of Casey's envy. "I'm starving. We haven't eaten since Fargo."

"Then let's eat!" Vanessa says. "I must take you to this fantastic place, Volare. It's downtown. The gnocchi is to die for."

"Do they have deep dish?" Dom asks.

Vanessa doesn't know how to tell Dom that a Michelin Star eatery doesn't serve the pizza of commoners. "Probably not," she says. "But we could do Lou Malnati's if you're into that sort of thing."

"I am very much into that sort of thing," he responds.

AT LOU MALNATI'S PIZZERIA. 8:30 PM.

"You going to finish that?" Dom asks as he points at an untouched slice of thick, cheesy pie on Casey's plate. She slides it over to him without a word, then takes a chug of her beer.

"My firm is just down the street from here," Vanessa volunteers. "There are several Stanford grads working with me, so it's really made the transition to corporate life easy. Here I am, fresh out of college, working my way up the ladder!" She is somehow oblivious to the fact that she started her climb on the top rung. When she doesn't get a follow-up question from Casey, she changes the focus to Dom. "Dom, I didn't ask, where are you working these days?"

"Oh, I'm not currently," he says with a mouth full of cheese and dough and satisfaction.

Vanessa doesn't know how to interact with someone who isn't even on the ladder, so she digs deep to find a conversation starter with him. "Um, last time I saw you, you were still in school at San Francisco State. Did you graduate yet?"

"Not yet," he says, ejecting a small chunk of crust onto the tablecloth. "Got a few more classes to go."

"Are you enrolled this semester?"

"Naw," he says between chews.

"Well, I just think that's wonderful you followed your sister out west, and now you both get to be in the same city," Vanessa says with her hand to her heart again. "Family is just so important."

Casey stares disgustedly at her brother, who has red sauce on his chin. She takes another chug of beer.

"So you said on the phone that you're going to see your dad," Vanessa says. "Where is he exactly?"

"Virginia," Casey answers bluntly.

"And your mom?"

"She's in Virginia, too. Can't ever be too far from that fucker."

"Oh!" Vanessa exclaims, changing the subject. "I must take you to this fantastic jazz bar called Andy's. It's just down the street. Are you into that sort of thing?"

"I am very much into that sort of thing," Dom says before shoving his loaded fork down his throat.

AT ANDY'S JAZZ CLUB & RESTAURANT. 10:30 PM.

A saxophonist with puffed cheeks blares his horn for the final measure of his solo. The crowd applauds. The rhythm section, consisting of three men with identical glasses, speckled beards, and ponytails, continues the song, and then the keyboardist begins what will be a meandering five-minute solo. Dom taps his fingers on the table along to the improvised melody as if he's a backup waiting for the bassist to pull a groin so he can have his moment to shine.

Vanessa leans over to Casey. "Don't you just *love* jazz?"

"Not really. It just keeps winding on and never resolves."

"Well, I just love it." Vanessa places her hand across her heart.

Casey tilts her chin up and lets the remaining suds trickle into her throat, then slams her glass down.

"If you want to get out of here, we should check out this fantastic speakeasy nearby."

"Does it have booze?" Casey asks with drunken snark.

Vanessa doesn't pick up on the sarcasm and gives Casey a playful nudge. "Of course it does, silly."

AT LULU'S SPEAKEASY. 11:30 PM.

"It's just, I don't get her, Ness," Casey slurs. She gulps her whiskey and continues her diatribe. "We were perfect for each other. Like soulmates and shit."

"Yes, you two were amazing together," Vanessa responds. "But break-ups happen, babe. I'm sure you'll find someone else out there who loves you as much as Kensington loves me."

"But that's the fuggin thing," Casey rebuts before taking a long intermission gulp. "I did have that. And I don't anymore. And it sucks ass and balls. And I want her back, but I can't have her because I'm cursed to misery and loneliness and pain until the earth is eventually swallowed up by the sun."

Vanessa looks around the room to see if she knows anyone. Casey continues.

"I mean, I drive up to Seattle and knock on her door, and do you know what she does? She acts like she doesn't know me. Like she doesn't even want to see me. I don't get it."

"Well it's probably because she has a girlfriend," Vanessa says casually. She takes a sip of her martini.

Casey's eyes flare as if Vanessa's words are a kilo of cocaine that she just inhaled through both nostrils. "WHAT?"

"Yeah, Angie probably felt weird seeing you because she has a girlfriend," Vanessa clarifies. She takes another sip, then realizes she just broke news that she didn't know was news. "Wait. You didn't know?"

"No, I didn't fucking know!"

Vanessa puts her hand to her mouth. "Oh, Case, I am soooooo sorry. I thought you knew. Everyone knows."

Casey erupts from the booth. "I have to go make a call." She immediately beelines for the door.

Dom returns after using the bathroom and finds Vanessa sitting there by herself. "What did I miss?"

OUTSIDE LULU'S. 11:45 PM.

Casey puts her phone up to her ear and paces up and down the sidewalk. *Hey, this is Angie. Leave a message. Beep.*

"Hey, it's me," Casey says calmly. She inhales, then proceeds to launch a punctuationless rant: "Your long-time girlfriend who you neglected to inform you had MOVED ON FROM leaving me to look like an ignorant dumbass thinking that there was still hope for us until VANESSA FUCKING MARTINELLI tells me because you didn't have the fucking decency you back-stabbing coward I hope you're happy goddammit I can't believe I spent so many years of my life with such a weasely ho who has great legs but no fucking courage fuck you rot in hell."

Casey shoves her phone into her pocket and looks up. Dom and Vanessa are standing in front of her, speechless.

"What the fuck do you two want?"

"Are you okay?" Dom asks.

"Am I okay? Am I *okay*? I just found out from a third fucking party that the love of my life is now the love of someone else's and I just can't even—"

"Okay, okay, okay," Dom says. "Just take a deep breath. Everything is okay. You're okay. We're all okay. Okay?"

"No I am not okay, Dom. I am fucking not." Casey screams an unintelligible expletive into the Chicago sky. Passersby stare at her, then resume living their lives. "I can't believe I didn't know she had a girlfriend. I'm apparently the only one on the planet who didn't. Aside from you, obviously."

Dom stands there awkwardly.

"Aside from you, *right Dom*?"

He somehow manages to stand there even more awkwardly.

"Wait. You *knew* about this?"

"Not the whole time," he sheepishly responds.

"*When* did you find out?"

"When we were in Seattle."

"In Seattle?! Like just a few days ago?! What?! How?!"

"Well, remember when I used the bathroom in Angie's place because I was super close to wetting my boxers?"

Casey stares directly into Dom's soul. She nods her head vigorously for him to continue, and Dom braces in anticipation of being a shot messenger.

"Well, um, she was there on the bed."

"On our *bed*?!" Casey nearly collapses.

"Yeah. Lying on top of the bed. Clothes on, though. I should stress that."

"What did she look like, Dom?"

"I, um, I only glanced at her."

"WHAT DID SHE LOOK LIKE DOMINIC?"

Dom tries to remember a woman he saw for less than a second. "Um, she was blonde."

"Ugh, she sounds like a bitch. Is she prettier than me?"

"Um, uh, you're my sister. There is no possible way I can answer that question."

"Arrrrg, this is unbelievable. Not only is Angie with some skank, whoever she is, but you knew about it and didn't fucking tell me." Casey walks around in vicious circles. Vanessa applies lip gloss and looks around to see if she recognizes anyone.

"I just figured you've been through a lot lately, and you weren't ready for this news," Dom explains.

Vanessa comes up and puts her arm around Casey. "We have to go to this fantastic tavern that's just around the corner."

AT GODFREY'S TAVERN. 12:15 AM.

Casey throws back a shot of cinnamon whiskey and calls for another one. The bartender motions with his hand in front of his neck to signal that he's cutting her off. Casey waits a moment, then tells Dom and Vanessa she needs to go to the bathroom. Vanessa says, "Kay, hun," and takes a sip of her martini as Casey stumbles off.

"So," Dom says to Vanessa. "Do you know any Midwest city chicks? A redhead, maybe?"

Vanessa ignores him and scouts the bar for a familiar face. Dom pivots. "I'm going to go check on Casey."

He leaves Vanessa at the bar and weaves his way to the women's bathroom. He knocks, calls Casey's name, waits, knocks again, and then cautiously opens the unlocked door. He peeks in timidly, hoping to find his fully clothed sister washing her hands and miraculously chipper, but all he sees is an unoccupied toilet and a lonely sink.

"Shoot."

Chapter 8

After Kip's Big Boy burgers one Sunday afternoon, when Dom and Casey were in high school, their father invited them to enter his study. He was often in this room, a sanctuary filled with leather-bound books and military artifacts. He instructed his progeny to sit down on two chairs in front of his desk and began to tell them a story about a serviceman in Vietnam named Perkins.

Perkins, Admiral King said, was a dope-smoking burnout from Des Moines who had his name called in the draft. When he arrived in Da Nang, he was a timid, confused eighteen-year-old. "I took him under my wing," Admiral King said proudly.

As the story goes, Perkins had never heard the good news of Jesus Christ, so Admiral King led him through the Sinner's prayer. "Dominic. Casey," their father said with a glint in his eye. "He accepted Christ into his heart that very moment."

The next morning, during the Tet holiday, when U.S. defenses were relaxed, the Viet Cong launched a surprise attack on South Vietnam. As the battle intensified, with gunfire ringing and smoke rising from mortar rounds, Admiral King dove on a grenade and saved the lives of eleven men. Perkins took a stray bullet from friendly fire to the back of the head and was dead before he hit the ground.

"He may have lost his life that day," Admiral King said to his teenage children. "But his soul is secure forever because he believed. And he wouldn't have believed if I had not shared the gospel with him. Yet you do not have to go to 'Nam to find lost souls, my children. They are right here in our midst."

Admiral King then instructed Dom and Casey to go through their suburban neighborhood and share the gospel with anyone who answered the knock at the door. "Your mission," their father said to them before they left the house, "is to seek and save the lost."

WALKING NORTH ON LASALLE STREET. 12:20 AM.

Dom and Vanessa move briskly on the sidewalk, weaving around drunk twenty-somethings and calling Casey's name.

"She could be anywhere," Dom says.

"She couldn't have gotten far," Vanessa assures him. She pulls out her phone and calls Casey, but there's no answer. She tries again.

Dom and Vanessa make a right at the corner but don't find any signs of her.

"I've never seen her like this," Vanessa says. "She was always so positive and confident. When she was a senior and I was a freshman, I followed her every move. She always knew where she was going. Now she's such a buzzkill."

"Yeah, her whole life has pretty much imploded," Dom says, swiveling his head around in hopes of catching sight of his sister before she commits a crime of passion. "She'll figure it out, though."

"All she needs to do to turn things around is just to tap into that good ole determination she used to show in the pool and keep moving forward."

"Yeah, for sure," Dom says. "But I hope she *physically* stops moving forward so we can find her. I think she's tapping into that determination to embark on a bloodthirsty sidequest for revenge."

Vanessa tries calling Casey again. No answer. She and Dom pass by a row of bars. A group of young women with heavy makeup and short skirts is standing on the sidewalk in front of a place called Roxy's. Dom approaches them.

"Excuse me, ladies," Dom says. "We're looking for someone. Pretty fit. Has her hair in a curly thing in the back. Wearing a grey Stanford sweatshirt. She might also be screaming at God or on the phone threatening to strangle someone named Angie. Have you seen her, by chance?"

The young women shake their heads and resume living their lives.

"I don't know what use it will be to try to chase her down," Vanessa says with frustration in her voice. "She's a smart girl. She can find her way."

"Yeah, but she's drunk on Fireball and vengeance," Dom responds. "I don't think the part of her brain that aced the SATs is steering the ship right now."

They make a right. Still no Casey. They walk south a couple of blocks, turn right, and end up back where they started. Still no Casey. Vanessa lets out an impatient groan. "She could be anywhere."

"She couldn't have gotten far," Dom assures her. "At least not on foot. Oh oh oh! Look! There she is!" Dom points up the street to the next block. He and Vanessa watch Casey stumble into the backseat of a cab, slam the door shut, and head north.

"Oh god, where is she going?" Vanessa's agitation grows.

"My guess is she told the cabbie to drive her to Seattle, but she probably only has enough cash on her to make it to O'Hare. O'shit! She's probably going to try and catch a flight there so she can whoop Angie's ass."

"At least she's safe," says Vanessa, oblivious to the fact that being an intoxicated young female in the back of a strange man's vehicle is not the ideal situation.

IN A CAB HEADING TO VANESSA'S TOWNHOME. 1:00 AM.

Vanessa convinces Dom that the best decision is to head back to her townhome and regroup. He doesn't see any other reasonable option, so he agrees. They hail a cab. On the way, Vanessa puts on lip gloss and tells the driver to turn the music up. "Omigod, I love this song!" she squeals.

IN FRONT OF VANESSA'S TOWNHOME. 1:30 AM.

Dom pays the fare, and they get out of the cab. He looks down the street and starts pondering the possibilities about where his sister might have gone. Maybe Casey will sober up, cool down, and then make her way back to the townhome, he hopes. And maybe along the way, she'll have met a couple of freckled University of Minnesota soccer players who are in town to see a Phish show and want to hang out, listen to him play guitar, and cuddle. No, he thinks, that's just silly and unrealistic. They would certainly be in town for an Usher concert.

He takes two steps and then sees the Jeep. The passenger door is wide open, so he bolts up to it. Casey isn't in there.

"I think we got robbed," Dom laments, putting his hands behind his head and exhaling.

"No way," Vanessa responds. "This is the premier neighborhood in Chicago. It's super safe."

"Then that means she was here!" Dom realizes. His excitement grows. "She must be back on foot now!"

"That's great. Makes a lot of sense," Vanessa yawns. "Hey, I'm going to head inside. It's super late. I'll leave the door unlocked for you!" She walks up her stairs without looking back.

Dom runs up the street until he reaches the intersection, then looks around. No Casey. He tries to put himself in the mindframe of his sister, a brilliant disaster, someone who just found out the ex they haven't gotten over has gotten over them. He concludes that Casey is single-handedly going to spike Chicago's crime statistics.

He turns back to get to the car so he can cover more ground before she goes on a spree. Then something catches his eye. He pulls up his sagging pants and hustles to get it.

There, resting in a bush like discarded drug paraphernalia, is the wide-open, empty keepsake box. He grabs it, sprints back to the Jeep, shuts the passenger door, pulls out his keys, and then gets behind the wheel to find his sister and the soccer players.

DRIVING LAPS. 1:45 AM.

Dom rolls up and down residential streets with his window down, calling for Casey. No signs of her. Then he turns onto West Wisconsin Street and sees a young couple walking and holding hands. He slows down and pulls up to them.

"Excuse me," he says. They stop and look at him curiously. "I'm looking for my sister. Pretty fit, wearing a Stanford sweatshirt. Might be foaming at the mouth. You haven't seen her, have you?"

The two lovers look at each other for a moment, grin, and then direct their attention back to Dom. The man responds, "Oh, you mean that crazy chick shoving a cross into people's faces and shouting 'Jesus is coming for you'?"

"Yeah, that's probably her," Dom says.

"We saw her over on Lincoln," the woman says, pointing in the direction the Jeep is facing. "Is she on meth?"

"No, heartbreak. Thank you." Dom hits the gas and heads east. When he gets to the intersection with Lincoln Avenue, he stops the car at a green light for a moment to decide which way to turn. Flashing blue and red to the left makes it an easy decision.

ON THE SIDEWALK BY SILVIO'S DELICATESSEN. 1:50 AM.

A cop car with its lights on is protruding onto Lincoln Avenue, forcing passing cars to change lanes. Dom makes a left toward it and miraculously finds an opening a few cars down. He haphazardly pulls into the tight spot and nearly forgets to shut off the engine before springing out of the Jeep.

He runs to the scene and finds Casey sitting on the sidewalk, her back slumped against the glass of Silvio's Delicatessen's locked front door. A muscly cop is crouched down having a very one-sided conversation, although Casey occasionally returns a sentence fragment in her semi-conscious attempt to explain her innocence.

Dom reaches the closed-eyed, mumbling Casey, and, short of breath, says, "It's okay, officer. She's my sister. I can take it from here."

The 6'6, 250-pounds-of-pure-meat agent of the state gives Dom a look of condescension, then remembers there are probably bigger crimes to worry about after midnight in the Windy City. So he stands up, tells Dom not to do anything dumb, and gets into his vehicle.

Dom struggles to lift his sister, who, despite only tipping the scale at 150 pounds, is dead weight. He manages to get her to her feet and escorts her to the Jeep, swaying side to side along the sidewalk with each step. He loads her into the passenger seat, buckles her in, and closes the door.

On their drive back to Vanessa's, Casey mumbles, "I just want this miserable story to end."

Chapter 9

"Sit down, Casey," Admiral King said to his twelve-year-old daughter.

She followed his instructions and climbed into one of the chairs in front of his desk, eagerly anticipating what her father was going to say next.

Admiral King then proceeded to tell her the story (again) of his heroism in Vietnam, the salvation he delivered to doomed soldiers in one bloody battle. "Do you understand the seriousness of what I've done?" he asked.

"Yes, Daddy, I do," Casey responded.

"Then today is a very special day. I have chosen to give you something of great importance."

Admiral King opened the top drawer of his desk and pulled out the emblem of his sacrificial bravery. He had received it at a ceremony in Washington, D.C. in 1970, an event attended by

President Nixon as well as the Marines he had saved. The cross was pinned to his chest by the Secretary of the Navy, who said, "You did more than save lives that day. You brought hope that we will win this war."

With the legend of his heroic sacrifice having been ingrained in Casey since she could remember, she was overjoyed that she had been ordained to receive it. Admiral King stretched his hand toward his daughter, the bronze medal resting in his thick palm. She slipped her tiny fingers under it, cupped it in her hand, and brought it closer to her face. She stroked the blue and white ribbon and memorized every contour and detail. To her, it was the most beautiful thing in the world.

"I'm trusting you with it, Casey," he said. "The Cross means everything to me. You must protect it."

"I will always keep it safe, Daddy," she promised.

VANESSA'S TOWNHOME. 10:30 AM.

Casey emerges from her room in her Stanford sweatshirt and tousled hair to find Dom and Vanessa sitting next to the grand piano in the first living room.

"Rise and shine!" Vanessa says with a smile that doesn't match the mood of the room.

Casey mumbles something inaudible in return, then plops down on a sofa next to a marble-lined wood-burning fireplace. She belches.

"How you feeling, sis?" Dom asks.

Casey belches again.

"I'm sorry I was the one to break the news about Angie and Brady," Vanessa says.

"Brady? Oh god, she even has a stupid name." Casey slumps into the sofa. While she moans and rubs her forehead, Dom gets up and walks to the bathroom.

"Brady is fantastic," Vanessa says with her hand on her heart. "She works at Microsoft, too. Super smart. And oh my god, she is *gorgeous*! Ugh, I'm jealous. Angie told me they're both heading to New York for this week's PCWorld Expo and then are going to spend the weekend in the Hamptons. Oh, didn't you two used to go to that convention together?"

"Every year," Casey responds. She feels like she's going to barf, and not from the hangover.

"Well, now Brady's the new Casey, I guess. It's so funny you had no idea about her, right? It's such old news." Vanessa giggles. "They've been together for like a year."

"Impossible," Casey says. "I've only been in San Francisco for six months." Then she remembers that she had been flying back and forth to San Francisco six months prior to her move so she could build her network, then connects the dots. She lets out an agonizing groan that echoes around the chandelier above her. Vanessa realizes she just broke news that she didn't know was news.

"You have got to be fucking kidding me," Casey says. "This can't get any worse."

"Well," Dom interjects as he returns from the bathroom. "I hate to be the one to break this news to you, but the Cross is missing. I found the box in a bush, but it was empty. And I checked your pockets last night. Also empty."

Casey slumps lower on the sofa. For more than half her life, she has kept the Cross, the invaluable family heirloom she promised to protect, securely in her possession. When she was younger, she wouldn't let Dom touch it, and barely even let him look at it. While living in the Stanford dorms, she kept it in a locked safe under her bed. The only time she had ever trusted someone else to handle it was when she told Dom to pack it with the rest of her things while he was helping her move from Seattle. But now, she feels a cocktail of guilt and shame for being the one to let it slip from her grasp. That is, before she could let it fly from her grasp in dramatic retaliation for the pain her father has caused her.

Dom quickly offers a proposed solution. "We can try to retrace your steps if you can remember where you went last night."

"I don't."

"We can just put our detective hats on then. Try to recreate your thought process and figure out where you might have gone."

"I didn't have a thought process. I blacked out."

Dom refuses to give up. "Then we can just aimlessly search and hope we get lucky."

Casey shrugs. "Let me go throw up first," she says, then belches.

"You two have fun!" Vanessa says with obnoxious bubbliness.

WALKING LAPS. 11:30 AM.

Dom and Casey walk south on North Orleans Street, east on West Menomonee, around the bend, and turn on Lincoln Park

W, frantically looking at every bush and into every trash can. I should mention that the Cross is 1.5 inches in diameter, and Chicago is 228 square miles.

WALKING LAPS. 1:15 PM.

The siblings shuffle up and down streets like drowsy zombies. At one point, they see a shimmering object, which provides momentary hope, but it turns out to be a crumpled Coors Light can. They've been walking for hours, and that's the closest they've come to finding the Cross, which is still 1.5 inches in diameter. Chicago is still 228 square miles.

WALKING LAPS. 2:30 PM.

"This is hopeless," Casey agonizes. She takes short, choppy, exhausted strides. With each waning step, her self-flagellating inner monologue picks up speed.

Dom doesn't want to add to her despair, so he continues to silently scan the vicinity.

"I can't believe I dragged us all the way here and then lost it. I fuck everything up."

"You're going through a lot, Case," Dom says compassionately. "This stuff happens."

"I'm cursed, Dom," she whines. "My life has been in a spiral ever since Dad marched out of Benihana and out of my life. That was the catalyst for my doom, like he pulled away his protection, and I was left to pay for my sins against a vengeful God."

Dom listens as he scours through a trash can, looks into a well-manicured bush, and moves on to the next. He's never been known for tenacity, but he'll search every street in Chicago if it means helping his sister.

"Maybe it's better this way. Maybe I don't deserve to confront him. Who am I anyway? This is a fitting ending, an anticlimactic sputtering conclusion that leads to the same result. I got rid of the Cross. That was the point all along. It's over. I need to accept it and move on."

They reach the corner of Wisconsin and Lincoln and wait at the crosswalk for a moment to let a Buick pass by. Dom rubs Casey's back in an attempt to ease her suffering, then they cross Lincoln Avenue toward Silvio's Delicatessen.

IN FRONT OF SILVIO'S DELICATESSEN. 3:45 PM.

Casey surveys the area where she was lectured by a Chicago PD officer, although she doesn't remember any of it. Pedestrians walk along the sidewalk, and a chubby guy waddles into Silvio's. Casey squints her eyes and tries to focus despite her throbbing headache. Maybe someone found it and took it to a pawn shop? Maybe they turned it in to the police? Maybe they—her eyes bug open and her heart starts racing. She sprints forward.

There, in the shadow under a sandwich board with the chalked words "Sil's Homemade Knishes – Get 'Em While They're Hot!" is the Cross. She rushes to pick it up. "I can't believe it," she exclaims. Dom thrusts his arms in the air like they had just won the Super Bowl, then high-fives a stranger. And then another. Then he goes into Silvio's to get a knish.

Holding the Cross securely in her hand, Casey feels relieved that she found it. And dismayed that she found it.

IN VANESSA'S TOWNHOME. 4:15 PM.

In the kitchen, Casey chugs a glass of water and then shoves a whole slice of organic wheat bread into her mouth while still gripping the Cross tightly in her right hand. Dom bathes his face in yellow Gatorade as the drink pours down his open hatch.

"I'm so glad you guys found your dad's thing!" Vanessa says, still in yoga pants and a tank top from her afternoon run.

"Thanks," Casey says. "I can't believe it. One in a billion shot."

"Well then maybe you can finally cheer up and get back to being the ole Casey I knew and loved," Vanessa says, unaware that finding the Cross merely returned Casey to her previous state, which is still not the ole Casey she knew and loved. Casey shoves another slice of bread in her mouth. "Hey, listen," Vanessa continues. "I have a super busy day at work tomorrow—*huge* client meeting—so you're leaving pretty soon, right?"

Casey swallows a wad of bread and realizes her welcome has worn out. "Oh, right. Yes. We're actually going to pack up and hit the road now."

"Aaaaawesome," Vanessa says. "I'm going to take a shower. It's been so great to see you both!" She prances out of the kitchen.

Casey looks at Dom. "Let's get the hell out of this city," she says, then devours another slice.

Chapter 10

The King household, like the others in their faith community, was built on solid biblical family values. As God had ordained, Admiral King was the leader, the provider, the protector. He offered the prayers before meals and administered the discipline. Mrs. King kept a lovely home, prepared the meals, nurtured the children, and was responsible for ensuring that the annual Christmas card went out before Thanksgiving.

With unparalleled regularity, the Kings attended Hollowsprings Church, a suburban congregation that met on a sprawling campus outside of Dallas, complete with specialized brick buildings, white steeples, sweeping foyers, and acres of parking. Every service, they sat in the front row of the sanctuary wearing their Sunday best, sang along to contemporary hymns performed by a robed choir, and absorbed every word from the tie-wearing pastor, who preached biblically-grounded sermons that emphasized pro-family, pro-life, and pro-anti-communist themes. Then, during the post-church lunches at Kip's Big Boy, Admiral King would quiz his children on what they learned and subsequently offer an exhortation to apply each message to their daily lives.

The Kings raised Casey and Dom on the firm moral principles delivered to humanity by the creator himself. Aside from the occasional Disney movie and benign pop song, the King kids were forbidden from consuming secular entertainment. As a holy alternative, they were permitted to watch films produced by Billy Graham's World Wide Pictures and listen to sanitized musical artists like Amy Grant, who Casey was shocked to learn was unknown to her elementary school classmates. (They must be blinded by secularitis, she reasoned.) Dom and Casey were allowed to watch Dallas Cowboys games, however, which provided the only relevant cultural touchpoint with their peers. Casey despised football.

Growing up, Casey believed the word "hell" was naughty unless it was used in the appropriate context of naming the place of unending torment filled with murderers and Democrats. She was kept from participating in her public elementary school's sex education program, and when encountering a picture of male genitalia in her alternative curriculum from Focus on the Family, felt a deep ickiness because she had seen a penis before her wedding night. (Later in life, she obviously discovered that biological factors were also at play in that repulsion.)

In eighth grade, Dom was caught with a cigarette and subsequently forced by Admiral King to smoke one Marlboro after another until he riotously vomited in the backyard. When he was caught with Nirvana's *Nevermind* during his freshman year of High School, he was required to write an essay on the perils of worldly compromise. He tried to bribe Casey to write it for him, to which she responded, "God is watching you, dumbass."

ON I-90/94 SOUTH. 4:45 PM.

Casey weaves through traffic under the towering Chicago skyline.

"Where are we going?" Dom asks.

Casey shrugs and hits the gas, then slams her brakes behind a semi-truck.

AT A SOUTHSIDE SHELL STATION. 5:15 PM.

After a quick gas stop, Dom racks the nozzle into the fuel pump as Casey returns from the convenience store with two Red Bulls and a bag of Nacho Cheese Doritos.

"Okay, I talked to my buddy Phil," Dom says, handing Casey's phone back to her. "He lives in Pittsburgh and says we can crash at his place. I know we'll be getting in late, but he said he'd wait up for us."

"Do I know Phil?"

"I don't think so. He's tight, though. Met him in college. We went to Reno once, and he got kicked out of an All-You-Can-Eat buffet for eating too much. Legend. We used to jam a lot at his place in San Francisco, but he moved back home to Pittsburgh to be closer to family."

"He sounds like a scrub. Is his place going to be a shithole?"

"No, it'll be really nice."

"Whatever," Casey says. "At least it's not an infested motel. Let's just get there."

PASSING THROUGH GARY, IN. 5:35 PM.

Through the passenger window, Casey zones out on industrial smokestacks feeding the grey sky. She puts Homer to her lips, pulls his head back, and swallows.

"So what's really in the PEZ dispenser?" Dom asks with concern.

"Xanax."

"Why do you keep it in a PEZ dispenser?"

"Because I didn't want you to know that I've been taking Xanax."

"Why not?"

"Because I didn't want you to know how weak I am."

Dom lifts his right hand from the steering wheel and places it on Casey's knee. She brushes it off.

PITTSBURGH, PA. 12:30 AM.

The dented Jeep's brakes screech as its overheating engine comes to a halt in front of a white house with a white picket fence. Casey and Dom sluggishly emerge from the vehicle, Dom grabs their bags from the back, closes the hatch, and they walk up a stone pathway toward the charming residence.

Dom gently knocks three times. They wait a moment in silence, then the door opens slowly. Greeting them is a lanky, dreadlocked turd.

"Holy shit, my homie! What are you doing here?!" he says in a loud whisper as he wraps his arms around Dom and slaps his back. Dom squeezes him tightly and slaps his back even harder. Casey zones out on a doormat that says "Home Sweet Home."

"Dude, it's been a minute. Fuuuuuuck," the turd adds, running his fingers through his dreadlocks. He turns to Casey. "Hey, I'm Phil!"

Phil extends his hand.

"I'm Dom's sister," Casey says, her hands remaining in her pockets.

"Does Dom's sister have a name?" Phil jests.

"No, she doesn't," Casey responds sharply. "Can we just go inside, please?"

"Fer shure," Phil says. He escorts them into the dark house. "Duuuuudes," he whispers as they walk from the entranceway and down a hallway illuminated by a single nightlight. "Welcome to my fuggin crib bros."

Phil escorts the King siblings to their room and says softly, "Make yourself at home. Dude Dommy, it's so sick that you're here." He gives Dom another back-slappy hug. "Alright, I'll let you homies sleep and I'll see you in the morning."

Dom and Casey scope out their room, which contains a single twin bed.

"I call big spoon," Dom says.

IN PHIL'S GUEST ROOM. 7:00 AM.

Casey wakes up alone on the edge of the bed. She sits up, sighs, rests her elbows on her knees, and runs her hand through her hair. She slowly rises to her feet, walks over to her toiletry bag, grabs her toothbrush, a half-rolled tube of toothpaste, and a pink hair tie, then leaves the room for the bathroom across the hall.

In the bathroom, without making eye contact with herself in the mirror, she pulls her hair back into a tight bun and twists the tie around until it's secure. She aggressively turns the faucet on, runs her toothbrush under it, adds toothpaste, puts it to her teeth, vigorously rubs it back and forth five times, puts it back under the faucet, taps it on the sink, snatches up the tube of toothpaste, and walks back to the guest room.

She throws the toothbrush and toothpaste into her toiletry bag, zips it up, and contemplates staying in the room by herself so she doesn't have to make small talk with Phil, who she's certain will give her a contact high while droning on about a bluegrass festival or something else she could give a shit about. But she's hungry, and that urge is strong enough to override her desire for solitude. Dom can keep that turd Phil occupied until after breakfast, she reasons. Then they can get back on the road.

Casey exits the room, walks down the hallway, and enters the main living space. Seated at the dining table are Dom and Phil. And a sullen woman who looks barely old enough to vote. And a silver-haired couple with cheesy smiles. And a preschool-age girl with a box of Honey Nut Cheerios in front of her.

"Who the fuck are you people?" is the first thing that comes out of Casey's mouth.

AT THE DINING TABLE. 7:05 AM.

"It's so nice to meet you, Casey," the silver-haired woman in a white sweater says as she stands up from her chair. "Dom has told us wonderful things about you. I'm Faye."

"Hi," Casey says with an obligatory wave.

The silver-haired man wearing a polo buttoned all the way to the top stands up, too. "And I'm Ray," he says as he reaches out to shake Casey's hand. Since she's standing ten feet away from him, he holds his hand outstretched until she can walk over to return the gesture. When she locks grips with him, Ray gives a firm and vigorous shake. Casey glares at Dom. He averts his eyes.

"Faye and Ray are my 'rents," Phil says.

"Huh?"

"My parents," he clarifies. "And this is my girlfriend, Misty, and our daughter—you want to tell Casey your name, baby girl?"

The little girl with pigtails blushes and hides her face behind the cereal box.

"She's just shy," Phil says. "This is Millie."

"Hi," is all Casey can say. Millie peeks out from the cereal refuge and then darts back to her hiding position. Misty doesn't react at all. Casey wonders if Misty is even breathing.

"Sit sit sit sit sit!" Ray says enthusiastically. "Can I interest you in a scrumptious bran muffin?"

"Um, sure," Casey replies, sitting down in a chair next to Faye and across from Dom. Ray plops the muffin on her plate. Faye fills a glass with orange juice and sets it in front of Casey. Millie darts out from behind the cartoon honey bee for a moment, then darts right back.

Casey looks around the space. On the walls are family portraits, a quilt hanging under a sign that says "Count Your Blessings" in cursive, and shelves adorned with black and white photos in gold frames. Toys are strewn across the living room, and in the corner is a large dollhouse. This isn't Phil's house, she ascertains. It's Faye and Ray's. Casey glares at Dom. He averts his eyes.

"We're so thankful you have come to visit," Faye says.

"Yeah it's so sick you're here, Dommy and Case!" Phil exclaims, putting his noodle arm around Dom's shoulder.

"I love your bracelet by the way," Faye says.

Casey looks down at her wrist, which is wrapped with a simple gold band. "Thank you. My ex-girlfriend got it for me. And now she's replaced me with someone else and is having a great time at the world's best tech conference in New York while all I have left is this stupid metal reminder that we once had something special. But it's dead now. Dead and gone. Never coming back."

"Oh, I'm so sorry to hear that," Faye says. She pours orange juice into Phil's glass, then changes the subject. "Was the bed comfy enough for you?"

"Yes," Casey lies.

"Oh, wonderful. I put fresh sheets on it as soon as Phil told us we were having guests. We were so happy to hear you were coming! How did you sleep?" Faye asks.

"Dom was snoring directly into my ear so I couldn't fall asleep for a while," Casey answers, her bran muffin lying untouched. She glares at Dom. He averts his eyes. Faye is not one for elaborations, yet Casey continues. "And then when I finally did pass out, I dreamed I killed God."

"Oh, oh my…" Faye adjusts her sweater nervously, hoping this is the end of Casey's story. It isn't.

"He appeared to me in the form of an eagle. I slashed his wings with an axe, severing them from his feathered torso. I watched the blood ejaculate from the stumps."

"Oh, oh dear," Faye gasps. "Anyone need more orange juice?" She scans the dining table nervously. No empty glasses.

"Then I swung the axe and lopped God's head off. Clean. Smooth. Like taking a warm blade to butter. His body slumped to the ground, and I stood over it. The river of blood trickled into the dirt as the torso slowly ceased convulsing, the upside-down head on the ground, beak agape, gasping for air until it took its last breath, releasing me from the torment of his sovereignty."

"I, I, I'm so sorry," Faye stutters.

She glances over at Millie in hopes that she's not absorbing any of Casey's content. Millie, with wide eyes, is locked in on every word. "That's a terrifying nightmare that is in no way real," Faye adds, her eyes on Casey but her words directed to Millie. "It's just a bad dream."

"No, I liked it," Casey says. She looks at Millie, who is still staring at her as if this is the first time she has ever been exposed to any content that's not from Focus on the Family, let alone a gory mental image of a decapitated bird god. Casey senses that she has taken a bite of Millie's innocence before taking a bite of her dry breakfast, so she backtracks, "Don't worry, little girl. It was just a dream. God isn't real."

Millie's eyes widen even more. Faye shuffles in her seat.

"I'm just kidding," Casey says.

Faye chuckles uncomfortably and looks for an empty glass to fill. Still none.

"He's real," Casey clarifies. "He's just a dick."

Faye quickly redirects her polite question to Dom in hopes that he will share a dream about God's wonderful love in clear enough language for Millie to receive. "And Dom, how did you sleep?"

"Great, thank you," he answers. He takes a sip of orange juice.

"So what are you doing for work these days, Dom?" Ray asks. Faye gives Ray a nod as if he is knowingly contributing to a wholesome discussion at the breakfast table. He has not paid attention to a single word spoken thus far.

"Nothing at the moment," Dom responds.

"Phil's also been out of work," Ray says. "Drug tests have gotten so strict these days. Did you lose your job, too?"

"Naw," Dom says. "I hit five numbers on the SuperLotto last year and won like a couple million bucks. So I bought a bunch of dotcom stocks because I knew Casey was into that stuff, but then I got bored and sold them for a pretty decent profit in February. Anyway, yeah, so I quit my job barbacking at T.G.I. Fridays, and I've been playing open mic nights and stuff. I'm getting a band together. We just landed a drummer named Keith. He's pretty chill."

"Whoa, really bro?!" Phil beams. "You're, like, super rich now?"

"Yeah, I guess," Dom responds. "It's nice to be freed up to pursue music, and to help Casey out while she gets back on her feet."

"That is certainly a huge blessing from the Lord," Ray interjects with a mixture of praise and suppressed longing for a lavish, unencumbered lifestyle. "You two are living in San Francisco, right?"

"Yeah," Dom says. "I was able to snatch up a sweet place in the Haight. The Grateful Dead used to live there."

"THE DEAD, BRO?!" Phil exclaims. "Dude, that is so illlllll." He gives Dom a bear hug and knocks over his orange juice, spewing it across the dining table. Faye hastily cleans it up with her napkin and then refills it. "Do you have an extra room, bro?" Phil asks with all seriousness. He hasn't been this energized since he pushed over a Sani-Hut at Woodstock '99.

Dom answers, "Yeah, three actually. Oh, wait, two since Casey moved in with me. But there's a den, too. I have drums and amps and a piano in there, but it could double as a bedroom. It's pretty big."

"It must be so flippin' rad living with your bro," Phil beams to Casey. "This dude is the fuggin sheeeeez."

Phil turns to Misty, who has been staring blankly through her sunken eyes the entire time. Still no sign of breath. "Babe, we should go back to San Fran and live with Dom and kick it with the ghost of Jerry Garcia and shit!" Misty doesn't blink.

"That would be so sick, bro!" Dom high-fives him. Phil high-fives him back. He and Phil clank their orange juice glasses and throw them down the hatch like shots.

Casey slowly chokes down her bran muffin and glares at Dom. He averts his eyes.

IN ~~PHIL'S~~ FAYE AND RAY'S LIVING ROOM. 9:30 AM.

Millie sits cross-legged on the carpet and plays with a Barbie. Dom and Phil take turns playing licks on an acoustic guitar. Misty watches Millie, or just stares blankly at her, it's hard to tell. Faye scurries around the living room picking up toys. Ray is outside mowing the lawn. And Casey is wondering how to get the hell out of here.

Dom slaps and picks a riff as Phil bobs his dreads back and forth. "Case, you gotta listen to this shit," Phil calls out to her from the couch. "Your bro is so tight at the guitar now. I was with him when he learned his first chord, and now he jams like a mofo."

"I need to go outside and make a call," Casey informs her brother, ignoring Phil's bromantic gushing. Dom changes keys and Phil loses his goddamn mind.

Casey opens the sliding door and steps out into the large backyard, which is home to a plastic Fisher-Price slide, an empty inflatable pool, and a hammock between two Sycamore trees. She pulls her phone out of her pocket, punches the keypad, and puts it up to her ear. *Hey, this is Angie. Leave a message. Beep.*

With that final unanswered call, Casey knows what she needs to do. She puts the phone back in her pocket, turns around, opens the slider, and enters the living room. Dom is slapping a new riff. Phil hangs on every note.

"Dom," Casey says. "Can I have a quick word with you?"

IN ~~PHIL'S~~ FAYE AND RAY'S GUEST ROOM. 9:35 AM.

In the guest room, the King siblings stand face to face next to the twin bed they shared the night before. "You know, Dom," Casey says. "I've been doing some thinking. And you're right. We should take our time on this trip. Go have some fun."

"Really?" he says. His face has the same gaping smile Millie's had when she got the dollhouse for her third birthday.

"Really. So, how about we make a little excursion to New York?

"REALLY?"

"Really. It's not like Dad is expecting us or anything. So why don't we go see the Big Apple, you know, since we're all the way over on this side of the country?"

Dom pumps his fists in the air and bounces around. "Yeah! That would be sick! Can Phil come with us?"

"No. I think he has to stay here and raise his fucking kid, you moron."

"Oh, true. But hell yeah, let's go to NYC! Wow. This is so unexpected. I'm amazed at your change of heart."

"Yeah," she says, nodding her head. "I really feel like I've turned over a new leaf."

Chapter 11

When you look back at the dotcom crash of 2000 to figure out what went wrong, it makes perfect sense.

Take, for example, the aforementioned Flooz.com, the Whoopi-endorsed digital currency that was marketed as a hip and innovative way to replace real money. The problem with creating a fake currency, though, is that people who rely on actual currency are a little hesitant to adopt it (namely, every human being on the planet). Since the dawn of human civilization, customers have given merchants tangible gold, silver, or government-backed marks in exchange for staples like goats, tunics, and flour. Economies are built on these kinds of trustworthy transactions. But by the time humans reached 2000, they thought that if a celebrity just announced something like "Hey, Flooz is a fun way for people to buy your shit", then merchants would simply sign up for the thrill. They didn't. Even the average consumer saw Flooz as redundant and complicated. As it turns out, the only loyal adopters turned out to be criminal organizations. They saw Flooz as a fun way to launder money.

In less than two years, Flooz.com burned through $50 million in venture capital and was forced to shut down operations. Nobody was left wondering why. But for some companies, like Casey's, the problem wasn't a naive idea with poor execution. It was bigger.

Casey had developed an innovative web-based grocery delivery system. While it was ambitious for the time, given that internet speeds could make it faster to walk across town and hand deliver a letter than send an email, her idea was solidly feasible.

While living in Seattle and working for Microsoft, she spent nights and weekends poring over market research and consumer psychology, working out her plan, crafting the business model, and developing the online platform and branding. Like many entrepreneurs, she was consumed with her vision. Then, with the encouragement of Angie behind her, she began making frequent trips to Silicon Valley to secure the necessary venture capital to bring her vision to market.

However, despite being a Stanford grad with direct experience in tech, she was denied meetings and, when she was able to land one, was teased and talked down to like she was a child. But she didn't quit. Eventually, she managed to secure a VC-friendly contract with Sequoia Capital, which gave them outsized control over her company. It was the best she could do.

She founded CityCart in the winter of 2000 and officially relocated to San Francisco in March. With her belongings still in boxes, the stock market bubble burst and, during the initial period of panic, the Sequoia Capital board informed her that they needed more of a professional (translation: male) CEO, pulled her funding, threatened her with expensive litigation, forced her to give up intellectual property rights, then discarded her like a floozy. Fucking tech bros.

On the day Casey officially filed for bankruptcy, she believed she no longer had a future. So she decided to settle the score with her past. That afternoon, she had an epiphany and proclaimed to an unassuming Dom, "Now is finally the time to deal with our father".

Then, wasting no time, she set out on a course for revenge, one that now includes another person who abandoned her.

"Vengeance is the Lord's," Admiral King once preached to his young children on a Sunday afternoon in his study. "It is a fearful thing to fall into the hands of the living God."

It's also a fearful thing to fall into the hands of a screwed-over genius with nothing left to lose.

I-76 EAST. 30 MILES OUTSIDE OF HARRISBURG, PA. NOON.

Dom, like an unsuspecting dog on the way to the vet, excitedly bounces around in the passenger seat. "East Coast city chicks aren't as hot as Midwest babes, but they're still pretty hot! We can meet some and then go rock our socks off. Oh man, I can't wait."

Casey, like a dog owner who is fully aware of what lies ahead, lets her loyal sidekick have his moment.

ON THE NEW JERSEY TURNPIKE HEADING
TOWARD THE LINCOLN TUNNEL. 3:00 PM.

"What's the first thing you want to do when we get there?" Dom asks eagerly. "What music venue do you want to go to first? The Wetlands? CBGB? Something cool I don't even know about?"

"There's actually a conference that should be wrapping up soon," Casey says. "I have to take care of a quick item of business, and then we can go find something fun to do."

"Solid," Dom says. He pants exuberantly as he looks out the window. Drool trickles down his chin. *It'll be over soon, buddy*, Casey says to him in her mind.

JACOB JAVITZ CONVENTION CENTER.
WEST SIDE, MANHATTAN. 3:30 PM.

The dented Jeep's brakes screech as its clanking engine comes to a halt on the busy street. Casey and Dom swiftly emerge from the vehicle, leave their bags in the back, and walk briskly toward the Javitz Convention Center. Dom looks up at the skyscrapers and says "Woooooooow".

"So there's a tech conference or something here?" he asks.

"Mhmmm," Casey responds. "The PCWorld Expo."

"Cool cool," Dom says, naively. "That sounds like something you'd be into. Have you ever been before?"

"A few times," she says, her eyes narrowing and a sinister smirk moving up her cheeks.

The siblings arrive at the main entrance of the convention center on West 34th Street. They stand in front of the large, modern glass structure for a while, and, to make the most of the wait, Dom gazes at the tall buildings and says "Woooooooow" like a skipping CD. Casey is laser-focused on the front doors like an assassin.

When the doors open, a throng of people wearing lanyards and satchels begins to appear. Casey, still with her relentless fixation, scans the crowd. Then she sees her. And *her*.

Angie is wearing a fitted turtleneck and khakis, her curly hair loose and flowing. Brady, contrary to Dom's memory, is actually a brunette and is fitted in a white button-up shirt and dark, bootcut jeans. She walks hand in hand with Angie, and Casey hates everything about Brady's outfit, vibe, and existence.

Angie and Brady stop on the curb, and Casey abandons Dom to make her move. She approaches the couple, appearing like an apparition in front of them, her face like that of a raging bull ghost. Angie is the first person to speak: "Holy shit! What are you doing here?!"

"What am *I* doing here?!" Casey shouts. "What the fuck are *you* doing here?" She motions to Brady, who has no idea what the hell is going on.

"Are you out of your mind?" Angie shouts back. Brady figures out who this disheveled, irate woman in a dirty Stanford sweatshirt screaming at her girlfriend is, but says nothing.

"You treacherous cowardly back-stabbing gutless smarmy bitch!" Casey snarls. "What in the ever-living fuck did I do to deserve to be treated like this?"

"I don't have time to deal with your crazy bullshit," Angie snaps back. "Get away from me."

Casey lunges at Angie and grabs her by the arm, causing Angie to buck her away, prompting Casey to swing an open palm at her face, slapping it across her cheek and cranking Angie's neck to the side. Angie swings her right fist in self-defense and connects with Casey's jaw. Casey, like a steel rhinoceros on PCP, doesn't flinch. She grabs Angie by the curls and pulls her head forward. Before Casey can rip her ex-lover's head off and hold it high in the air like a victorious warlord, an arm wraps around her from behind, pulling her back. As she's apprehended, she releases her grip on Angie's hair, strands of curls still stuck to her shaking palm.

Dom uses all his might to keep his sister contained, but her squirrely strength enables her to wriggle free. Onlookers gawk. "You lying disrespectful snatch!" Casey screams as she lunges forward again.

"Get out of my life!" Angie screams back. Brady reaches her arm around Angie's shoulder and pulls her away. Dom does the same to Casey. Onlookers gawk as much as they've ever gawked. Brady comforts the ruffled Angie and leads her back toward the convention center.

Then Angie stops and turns to Casey.

"You know, you've been leaving me all these unhinged messages accusing me of abandoning you, Casey," Angie says with a red face and tears welling in her eyes. "But you left me long before you moved to the Bay. I got none of your attention once you started your business. You left me for your ambition, Casey. All I did was give you a nudge out the door." Angie turns away, Brady gives her a kiss on the cheek, and the two women disappear into the crowd.

Dom guides his sister in the opposite direction, toward the blocked-off street in front of the main doors. "What the hell, Casey?" he says sternly. "Have you gone crazy?"

She huffs and puffs, and with tears streaming down her cheeks, shakes her head violently and storms off. Dom chases after Casey. She speeds up.

"Get the hell away from me!" she shouts.

"Casey, what are you doing?!"

"I'm just being an agent of God's justice since he's nowhere to be found."

"That's insane!" Dom exclaims. "You need to let go. Revenge isn't the answer."

Casey pivots around on a dime.

"What do you want? Do you want me to be like you, huh? A blob who just passively flows with the waves?"

"I'm not passive," Dom says sternly. Casey is caught off guard by his pushback, but she stands her ground.

"Yes. You. Are. You've just been along for this ride because you have nothing better to do."

"No," Dom responds with calm force. "I went on this trip to be here for you. I've looked up to you my whole life, Casey, but you've been spiraling out of control. And you're dragging everyone else into your mess. It breaks my heart, sis."

Casey huffs. "You know what? Fuck you, Dom," she screams as she jabs her finger into his chest. "I don't need you. Or anyone. Fuck this shit. Angie was just a warmup. I'm going to Virginia to take on the final boss. Alone."

Casey hustles to the Jeep, gets behind the wheel, and peels out of the spot while Dom stands there in shock. When he finally accepts that she's not coming back, he sits down in front of the convention center next to a flock of pigeons pecking at the ground. He has no idea what to do next, so, like the pigeons, he just shuffles around on the sidewalk.

Chapter 12

When Casey chased after her father in the Benihana parking lot on the night she and Angie revealed the true nature of their relationship, she believed, deep within her soul, that the man she had loved her whole life would understand her if only he could see the situation from her perspective.

"Dad, please," she begged him as he moved away from her. "Please don't leave."

With the calloused resolution of someone whose character has been forged by the atrocities of war, Admiral King stared his daughter down and coldly said to her, "You have rejected your creator. He made you for a purpose, Casey, and you are throwing that away to run after your passions."

"No, Dad, that's not what I'm doing!" she pleaded.

"Silence!" he commanded as he pointed his finger at her. "You are not my daughter anymore." Then he directed his attention to

Casey's mother, the lone witness to the event, and said sternly, "Mary, get in the car." She didn't move. His anger boiled, and he raised his voice. "Mary, get in the damn car. Now!"

With tears welling in her eyes, she obeyed her husband. Then Admiral King turned his face away from Casey, got into the vehicle, and drove out of her life.

I-95 SOUTH. PASSING BY PHILADELPHIA, PA. 7:30 PM.

The lights of the City of Brotherly Love's skyline disappear behind the trees lining the interstate as the Jeep's temperature gauge spikes to the red zone. Steam rises from the mangled hood, accompanied by a knocking sound.

Casey glances at the blinking lights on the dashboard, then presses the accelerator.

SOMEWHERE SOUTHWEST OF WILMINGTON, DE. 8:30 PM.

The engine's power wanes, and the fuel light comes on. Casey exits I-95 and pulls into a gas station parking lot. She puts $20 into the tank and gets back on the road.

APPROACHING THE BALTIMORE, MD METRO. 9:15 PM.

Exhausted, and with the engine pinging, knocking, smoking, dying, Casey decides to pull off the interstate and rest her eyes for a minute. She guides the Jeep to an empty parking lot nestled under towering oak trees, loses consciousness, and doesn't wake up until daylight breaks.

ENTERING SUBURBAN WASHINGTON, DC. 7:00 AM.

Casey returns to the road, but doesn't make it far. With a final hissing, sputtering gasp, the Jeep stalls, and Casey is forced to pull off the shoulder of I-95. She slinks out her door, pops the hood, and waves away a cloud of hot vapor with her hand.

A Ford F-150 pulls up behind the smoking Jeep, and a middle-aged man in a plaid button-up shirt tucked into blue jeans with a large belt buckle walks up to Casey. "You okay, miss?" he says with a southern drawl.

Casey, with bloodshot eyes, motions to the carnage in front of her. The man senses her distress and calmly inspects the engine compartment.

"Sorry to be the bearer of bad news, but it looks like your radiator is shot," he informs her.

"Hmmm," is all Casey can respond with.

"Yeah, looka' here." He points at a light brown cylinder impaling the radiator. "It's a goshdarn deer antler shard. My word, I never seen nothing like that. This puppy's toast."

Casey puts her hands behind her head and exhales in despair.

"Want me to call you a tow?" the hick Samaritan asks.

"No," Casey replies. "I'll just get a cab."

"Alrighty then. Best of luck to ya," he says. He moseys back to his F-150 and returns to the road as Casey watches the steam from the deceased vehicle dissipate into the cool morning air.

ON THE SHOULDER OF I-95. 20 MILES FROM ARLINGTON. 7:30 AM.

When the cab pulls up, Casey grabs the keepsake box from the passenger seat, slings her bag over her shoulder, and climbs into the backseat. Her winding, frustrating journey has led to this moment, the final descent, the culmination of her vengeful fantasies. She just didn't expect to be this war-torn heading into the battle.

"Where to, lady?" the cabbie asks in broken English.

Casey clutches the keepsake box against her chest. "Arlington National Cemetery."

Chapter 13

"Death comes for all of us," Admiral King said to his eight-year-old daughter one night after bedtime prayer. "It's coming for me, and one day, it will come for you too. And it's final. The question is, until the day you die, are you going to be faithful to the Lord?"

"Yes, Daddy," Casey responded, gripping her Care Bears blanket tightly. "I will."

ARLINGTON NATIONAL CEMETERY. 9:00 AM.

Rows of white headstones stretch out as far as the eye can see, over 400,000 memorials for soldiers known and unknown dotting 639 acres of rolling hills covered by lush green grass. Casey King stands before the only grave that has significance to her, the one of her father, the man she revered as a child, feared as a teen, avoided after he rejected her, and has hated since the day he died.

Under the grey Virginia morning sky, she stares at the white marble headstone engraved with these words:

Paul H. King
Admiral, United States Navy
Born: December 25th, 1940
Died: July 4th, 1997
Faithful to his country and God
Recipient of the Navy Cross

As she rehearsed so many times in anticipation of this moment, Casey pops the silver latch and opens the keepsake box, revealing the bronze Cross, a gift once given by a commanding father to his devoted daughter.

She slips her fingers under the Cross, cups it in her palm, then brings it close to her face. She strokes the blue and white ribbon and fixates on every familiar contour and detail. To her, it's the most painful thing in the world.

When she received it as a child, she eagerly shared the news of the gift with anyone who would listen. Before big swim meets, she'd squeeze it and pray to God with fervor that he'd empower her body. At night, she would kiss it before climbing into bed. She loved the Cross because she loved the one who gave it to her. But after being deserted in a dark parking lot, left with the haunting abandonment that has eaten at her ever since, she can only feel sadness when she holds it. The symbol of heroism has become a reminder of loss. And now, she's ready to lose it forever.

She clutches the Cross in her right hand and cocks her arm back, coiled to launch forward and slam it down. But her incessant fantasy of hurling it to the ground above Admiral King's rotting corpse, fueled by the rage of a discarded daughter, suddenly vanishes like a bursting bubble. Taking its place is something else, something much stronger: the deep agony of a despairing daughter.

Her grief overpowers her. Casey's arm drops to her side, limp, her tight fist opening involuntarily. The Cross falls gently to the grass, making a soft sound as it lands on its resting place six feet above the one who earned it.

There is no shouting, no explosive gesturing, no verbal assault. "You left me," is all Casey can say, her voice wavering, tears trickling down her cheekbones. "I believed you. Trusted you. Followed you. And then you were gone." She breaks down and falls to her knees.

With the veil of vengeance lifted from her eyes, her illusion that she could ever settle the score with her father has vanished with him. All she has now is an aching emptiness inside her, the echoes of a piece of herself buried deep in the ground. Gone, forever. And for the first time in her life, she has no idea where to go next.

"What am I supposed to do?" she whimpers between sobs. She falls forward with her hands stretched out like she used to do as a young child, as if her dad would scoop her up in his arms and squeeze her tightly. But this time, the only thing wrapping around her is the air. She falls forward to the ground and buries her face in the grass. With a thick layer of earth separating her from the one who used to be her refuge, bawling, she repeats: "What am I supposed to do now?"

In that moment, Casey feels a buzzing on her hip. She rises to her knees, wipes her eyes, sniffles, reaches into her pocket, and pulls her phone out. She glances at the caller ID, presses a button, clears her throat, and puts the device to her ear. "Hey," she says with a hushed tremble.

"Hi, sweetie," her mother responds. "Are you there now?"

"Yes," Casey replies. She wipes her eyes again. "How did you know?"

"Dom called and let me know you were coming to Virginia. And he just called me to tell me you were going there by yourself."

Casey sniffles and wipes her nose. "I'm so alone, Mom. I'm stranded here. I don't know what to do."

"Stay where you are," her mother replies. "I'm coming for you."

Chapter 14

Admiral King died on Independence Day in 1997, two weeks after he left a distraught Casey alone in the Benihana parking lot.

It happened on a Friday morning. Mary walked into his study to bring him a cup of coffee and found him lying face down. She rushed to resuscitate him, but he was already gone.

The autopsy later revealed that he had succumbed to a ruptured cerebral artery, which triggered a hemorrhagic stroke like a stray bullet from friendly fire. He died before he hit the floor.

Admiral King's funeral service was held at Arlington National Cemetery on a balmy summer afternoon. His casket, draped with the American flag, was escorted by an honor guard. A 21-gun salute was performed, followed by the solemn bugle call of "Taps." Then the flag was folded, and an officer presented it to Mary and Dom. Casey had refused to attend.

IN MARY'S BACKYARD. SEMINARY HILL, ALEXANDRIA, VA. LATE MORNING.

Vibrant pinks, purples, and greens pop through misty droplets dotting the backyard flora. Beams of light poke through brooding clouds hovering overhead, and two towering white oak trees shade the grass beneath them. The trickle of a small creek accompanied by a symphony of chirping birds fills the air.

Casey rocks back and forth on a wooden swing and takes a sip of steaming tea. Her mother relocated from Texas to this home in Alexandria shortly after the death of her husband so she could be close to his grave, and this is the first time Casey has seen the Edenic backyard garden Mary has cultivated in his absence.

A gentle breeze picks up as Mary appears. She sits down beside Casey on the swing and rests her hand on her daughter's thigh. "I just got off the phone. Your Jeep was towed to a shop here in town," Mary says. "And they'll be able to get the radiator fixed by tomorrow morning."

"Thank you," Casey replies meekly. She takes another sip of her tea.

"How are you doing?" Mary asks as she softly rubs Casey's thigh.

"I don't know what I'm feeling right now," Casey responds. "It's just been a lot lately." She pushes the ground with her feet and propels the swing back, then lets momentum take over.

"Yes, it has," Mary affirms, swinging beside her.

"I've screwed my life up, Mom. It's like I've spent the last three years digging my own grave. Now I'm just lying in it, waiting for someone to come by with a backhoe and cover up my remains."

"You haven't screwed your life up, Casey," Mary responds. "You're a resilient person. You always have been. You'll make it through this."

Casey doesn't believe her. "It just feels like this is the end of the road. I don't know what I'm going to do next."

"You don't need to have the answers right now," Mary says. "But I know you'll figure out where to go. Be patient with yourself."

Casey hangs her head. "I just haven't felt like myself for so long. Like I've been irreparably damaged. A shadow of what I once was, doomed to carry on with a curse for the rest of my life. I don't trust my decisions. I don't have any hope that anything will work out. And this is all his goddamn fault."

"Why do you think that?" Mary asks.

"Because he set the path for my whole life. Every decision I ever made was with him in mind. I trusted him. Followed him. *Obeyed* him. And then he fucking disowns me? All of his claims that he loved me were complete bullshit. All of his claims that he would be there to protect me were entirely conditional. He was *family*. And, just like that, he was gone. Forever. Leaving me with nothing but a lingering sense of being defective, of being a sinful rebel. He gave me a house of cards and called it a fucking fortress. And he's not here to help me as I deal with its collapse."

With her hand still affectionately on Casey, Mary responds, "Your father is responsible for a lot of pain in your life, and your anger against him is justified. He gave you a simple framework for understanding a complicated world. And he tried to shape you into his image. You had to tragically discover that the worldview he created in your young mind, the one you received and believed in, doesn't work. And that you don't fit the box he tried to keep you in. I'm sorry you've had to experience that. It's confusing, and it's heartbreaking."

"Who are you to talk?" Casey says sternly. "You let it happen. You just stood there silently and didn't stop him."

"You're right, Casey. I understand why you're angry with me, too. I stayed silent when you needed me most, and for that I am sorry. Your father had his way of keeping me quiet, and as much as I was there for you, that wasn't enough. I'm deeply sorry for that."

Casey watches the liquid in her mug ripple as she slowly swings back and forth.

"You're grieving, Casey," Mary continues. "And grief is a heavy weight to carry. It clouds our souls and dims our view of the future. But you're confronting your grief head-on, and I'm thankful you're doing that. It's the first step toward your restoration."

"Yeah, but I don't feel any better. I drove across this god-forsaken country to rid myself of the unrelenting haunting of my dick father. But nothing's changed. He's still dead, and I'm still mopping up the mess I'm in."

Mary replies, "It will be a while before you find peace. It's a process. A long one. So be patient with yourself. Your father's death is not all you've been grieving."

Casey's eyes squint with curiosity.

"You've also been grieving the death of the life you expected to have," Mary says. "A vision for a future that is no longer possible. That's a real loss, too, even if it never actually existed."

"I got screwed," Casey says, her anger beginning to boil.

"I love you, Casey," Mary replies. "You have been wronged. That's true. But it's not helping you to be consumed by your rage over it."

Casey dismounts from the swing and rises to her feet. "Who do you think you are?" she snaps back, pointing her index finger squarely at Mary. "I have every right to be angry!"

"Yes, you do," Mary gently responds. "I'm not disagreeing with that. What you've experienced has been unfair. But you're letting your anger control you, and that has been amplifying that pain. It's also been spreading chaos to everyone around you."

Casey shakes her head and paces around the patio. "My anger is the only thing that makes me feel like I'm not a weak little girl."

"I understand that. But if you can release it, you'll find that you are stronger than you realize."

"Yeah, well, how am I supposed to do that?" Casey asks incredulously as she paces.

"Coming here is the first step in your healing. I'm proud of you for having the courage to face the ghosts of your past. Too many people just try to ignore their pain and push forward, but that doesn't work. You're a forward-moving person, Casey, but right now the only thing you can do is let yourself feel the grief."

"I need to go lie down," Casey responds, the feeling of poisonous sadness flowing through every part of her being. She walks across the yard to a hammock suspended between the two oak trees. She climbs in and sways from side to side, with misty tears in her eyes, gazing up at the blurry sky until it gives way to darkness.

AT MARY'S DINING TABLE. EVENING.

For dinner, Mary prepares Casey her favorite childhood meal, cheeseburger casserole, a dish that Casey would often make for herself in college whenever she longed for southern comfort and a sense of home. She hasn't tasted it in years.

At the dining table, while Casey somberly picks at the leftovers on her plate, Mary breaks the silence: "What's going on in that brilliant mind of yours?"

"I wish I didn't have to go through all of this," Casey responds, poking at an elbow macaroni like it's a pin cushion. "I'm just wondering what I could have done differently."

Mary's heart breaks for her despondent daughter. "You made the best decisions you could with the information you had at the time. I hope you see that," she says. "You can't change what's happened to you, Casey. I'm sorry."

"Then I wish I could have my mind erased so I could forget it all."

"Then you would lose what you've learned. And that's what you need for your next chapter. You can't go back in time, you know that, but you can come to terms with your past, and you can move forward with a new understanding."

"What's there to understand? I was just a naive idiot," Casey volleys back. "End of story." She stabs the macaroni.

"No, Casey," Mary corrects her. "You're stopping the story short."

"What the hell does that even mean?"

Mary pushes her chair back and rises to her feet. "Come with me. I have something I think you're finally ready to see."

Chapter 15

Growing up, Casey looked to her father as one who had all the answers. He had a commanding presence, an awe-inspiring aura, and an unwavering confidence in his convictions. He had waded through the swamps of war with a firm resolution and carried that forward in the way he led his family. He provided for them, instructed them in the truth, and created a structure of security and order. He inspired Casey to push herself, to relentlessly move toward her goals, and to sacrifice herself for the greater good. Admiral King was her North Star.

Casey felt safe in the clear direction of her father and obeyed his every command, even when her young mind didn't understand. "The rebellious," Admiral King often said, "deserve the rod of discipline. But God rewards those who trust him." Casey believed that in the deepest part of her soul.

Mary, however, was not given the same respect by Casey, who saw her mother as a bleeding heart lacking the precision necessary to articulate divine truth to a lost world. On one occasion, when Casey was ten, Mary took her to a hospital ward to sit bedside with AIDS patients. Mary held their frail hands, conversed and prayed with them, fetched them water, and called for nurses as needed while Casey sat in a chair watching.

"Why are we doing this?" Casey whined, uncomfortably looking at a sore-covered, dying man in the bed in front of her. "He can't even talk. How do we know if he gets saved?"

"God's love is deeper than words," Mary answered.

Casey, parroting her father, bluntly replied, "The unrepentant will face God's wrath."

"There's more to the story than that," Mary responded.

Casey volleyed back, "If that was true, then it would be in the Bible."

It's not that Casey ever hated her mother. She always could see the good in her and certainly felt her love. But Mary was never assertive enough, never certain enough, and, unlike Admiral King, never one for Casey to anchor herself in.

Then one day, when Casey was twelve, she approached her father's study and caught the tail end of an argument between him and Mary, one of many conflicts behind closed doors that she was aware of but never privy to.

"You have no grounds to speak," Casey overheard Admiral King bark at his wife. "You must submit."

As Casey entered the study, the room fell silent. Mary nodded without saying a word, and Admiral King motioned to the door with his head. Mary departed.

"Sit down, Casey," Admiral King said as his wife left the room. He proceeded to tell his daughter the familiar story of his heroism in Vietnam, the salvation he delivered to doomed soldiers in one bloody battle. "Today is a very special day," he said. "I have chosen to give you something of great importance."

That was when he presented the Cross to Casey, who received it with joy. Mary somberly wept outside the study.

IN MARY'S HOME. EVENING.

Mary leads Casey down a hallway and opens a door, revealing a flight of stairs into a dark room below. She takes the first step and flips a light switch, and Casey follows closely behind her.

"I've kept your father's things down here since I moved into this house after he died," Mary says as they descend. "I have his books, his uniforms, and all his prized possessions."

When they get to the bottom of the stairs, Casey surveys the cold basement around her. Artifacts of a man she once considered to be her hero fill the space. Boxes containing the leather-bound volumes that used to line the shelves of Admiral King's study, a bronze bust of General Patton on an antique dresser, and a bag of golf clubs leaning next to it. "I don't have anything left that connects me to him anymore," Casey says. "Just memories that I hope will fade away."

"Your father was flawed," Mary says as she moves toward the dresser. "Not evil, but deeply flawed. He was confident in what he believed to be true and good. And he wouldn't consider anything else." She stops and looks directly at Casey. "So what I'm about to show you is going to be hard to see."

Casey feels a sinking sensation in her stomach. She braces herself for what's coming, her muscles tense, her heart beating rapidly. Mary lifts a small mahogany box with a gold latch off the dresser and hands it to her daughter.

Casey holds the box, looks down at it, and then back up at her mother with a mixture of apprehension and intrigue. Mary motions with her eyes, and Casey implicitly understands what to do. She cautiously disengages the latch and opens the top. There, secured in the center, is the bronze Navy Cross. Casey feels a jolt of adrenaline radiate through her fingertips like she's just seen a ghost.

"Look at it closely," Mary instructs her.

Casey slips her shaking fingers under the Cross, cups it in her palm, and brings it close to her face. Even though it has been in Casey's possession for years, and she has studied every feature, this time, it looks different in a way she can't identify.

"You went to the cemetery and got it?" she asks with confused sadness.

"No," Mary responds. Casey is perplexed, not comprehending how she could possibly be holding it in her hand. Mary puts her arm on her daughter's shoulder. "The one you left at the grave isn't the real Cross."

Casey inhales sharply. Stunned, she reexamines the medal in her quivering hand, the object that once brought her awe, that encapsulated bravery and sacrifice, the artifact that has bound her to the haunting presence of her father. Her eyes shoot back to her mother.

"He gave you a replica," Mary says. "I begged him not to, but he insisted."

Casey's face turns pale. She feels herself falling straight down as if the floor beneath her feet suddenly gave way. But she, in her flesh, remains standing. It's the foundation of her reality, what she has believed to be true, that has collapsed.

In shock, Casey can barely get this one word out: "Why?" When she says it, her lips quake from surprise and surging anger.

"The Cross was the summation of his purpose, the symbol of his mission. He needed to ensure it was protected, so he couldn't let the real one escape his grasp. It meant everything to your father. Even, sadly, more than the truth."

"And more than his daughter, apparently," Casey painfully concludes.

"But he's gone now," Mary responds. "And with him, the imitation Cross you inherited."

Casey can't formulate a word. Her rage swells.

"I know this adds to your pain," Mary says. "And I know this raises a lot more questions."

Casey's body tenses up, and she does what she had been unable to do at her father's grave—she hurls the Cross down to the ground. It bounces along the concrete floor, clanking as it slams into the wall on the other side of the basement.

"Why didn't you tell me I had a bullshit copy before?" she scolds Mary. "What the hell is wrong with you?"

"You weren't ready then," Mary calmly says. "You wouldn't have believed me if I told you when he was alive, and he would have vehemently denied it. He had the power to convince you of that. I had to wait until after he died. This is the only way you could hear my voice, and finally be able to know the truth."

"That's messed up," Casey says. "I cannot believe this is happening." She compulsively adjusts her bun, her heart throbbing. She feels like she's going to pass out, so she takes deep, measured breaths.

"I hear you, Casey," Mary says. "I know this news compounds your loss. But I want you to be able to move beyond your father without having to hate the role he played in your life. Please understand that what your father gave you, as distorted as it was, has set the table for you to receive the real thing, this time with a completely new meaning."

Casey glares at her mother. "I don't want anything to do with it ever again." She turns and runs up the stairs, leaving Mary alone in the cold basement.

IN MARY'S GUEST ROOM. MIDDLE OF THE NIGHT.

Lying awake in a seemingly eternal night, Casey is engulfed in darkness and silence. Even though she's in her mother's house, it's a foreign place to her. And even though Mary is in her bedroom down the hall, Casey feels completely, terrifyingly, alone.

As she lies on her back, a storm of visions fills her agitated mind. A visual of Angie and Brady taking a bath together in the Hamptons blends into an abandoned Dom purposelessly trodding through the streets of Manhattan, which gives way to an even more haunting scene: the gravesite of her father, his tombstone white and prominent, his name permanently etched into the marble memorial.

Casey envisions herself taking a shovel to the earth above his resting place. She presses her foot on the spade and digs deeper and deeper until she strikes something solid. She clears the remaining dirt, revealing a mahogany casket that stores Admiral King's remains. In her mind's eye, she climbs out of the hole she's dug and watches the wooden tomb, waiting for it to creak open. But it doesn't. There is no resurrection, not even in her imagination.

She feels the damp traces of grief cooling the sides of her face. But with each passing trickle of tears, the vision of the cemetery fades, and appearing in its place is something else, something warm and comforting: her mother's image. Mary's kind and inviting eyes rest atop her soft cheeks, which are framed by her long, gray hair. It's the face of ancient youth, the distinguished features of a woman that Casey had dismissed her whole life. Mary smiles, and, gradually, the guest room begins to brighten.

Casey slowly turns to her side. Then she notices the faint glow of dawn peeking through the curtains.

Chapter 16

"Mommy," twelve-year-old Casey said as she bounced out of her father's study. "Look at what Daddy gave to me!" She held the Cross up to Mary's face.

"One day, you will know the truth," Mary responded with red, puffy eyes. "And the truth will set you free."

IN MARY'S BACKYARD. MORNING.

Casey swings back and forth, looking down at the mug between her legs. She stirs the tea with her finger but doesn't take a drink.

"Were you able to sleep last night?" Mary asks, sitting close beside her.

Casey shakes her head and doesn't make eye contact. "All night I was thinking about how crazy this whole situation is.

How could he justify his deception? How could he do that to a *child*?"

"There is no excuse for it," Mary says. "He knew what he was doing. He refused to be convinced otherwise."

Casey gives an affirming nod. "That piece of shit control freak. I just can't believe I couldn't see it. Was I really that dumb?"

"No, you weren't dumb, Casey. You were so young when he gave it to you. And you trusted him." Mary rests her hand on Casey's. "There's no way you could have known."

"I should have figured it out. I'm just that gullible, apparently. I've spent all this time blaming him for my woes. I should point that finger at the mirror. Now I have to live with the guilt of my stupidity, too."

"No, you don't," Mary contends. "You can be freed from that."

"How?" Casey scoffs.

"Forgiveness."

Casey shakes her head and dismissively huffs. Another trite Christian virtue, she thinks.

"I can't forgive him," Casey says sharply. "Fuck him."

"No, not forgive your father," Mary responds. "The person you have to forgive is yourself, Casey. You followed what you believed to be true, and followed it wholeheartedly. But those beliefs failed you. You can see that now. And there's no returning to them. The only way you can move forward is by releasing your past self from the blame. It's hard to do that, I know, but it's the only way to find life on the other side. Don't let your father write the end of the story."

Casey scoffs. "I think the credits started rolling when he was lowered into the ground. I can't get back at him, and I've tried. End of story. He wins."

"You're right, you can't get revenge," Mary says. "Even if you could, it wouldn't change anything. And you'd be no better than him. Vengeance is not the way, Casey. But that doesn't mean he wins."

"I don't get what you're saying." Casey looks up at her mother with skepticism.

Mary is silent for a moment, then dismounts from the swing. Casey watches her as she opens the sliding door and enters the house. Casey waits with confused anticipation, unsure of what her mother is doing and even more unsure if she wants to know.

A few moments later, Mary emerges from the house and walks to the swing. She stretches her arm out, and in her palm is the mahogany box containing the Cross. Casey snorts and rolls her eyes. "If you want to write the ending of the story," Mary says, "then take the Cross with you. Only this time, with an entirely new narrative that transcends what it meant when your father gave it to you."

"I don't want it," Casey argues. "It's tainted."

"I understand why you think that," Mary responds. "But that's only true if you choose to see it that way. And I beg you not to. Your grief over what he's done will never entirely leave you, but its power over you can be released. Trust me. Take the Cross with you, Casey. This time, it's not being given to you by a father who wants you to remember that he saved people from the fires of war. It's being given to you by a mother who wants you to remember that your old life is dead. And that you are now free to live a better one. Take the Cross as a symbol of your death and resurrection. If you can do that, you'll be able to see that the past was not a waste. It was a necessary stage in your evolution."

Casey has never heard Mary speak like this, with such conviction and direction. Ever since she could remember, her mother's words were always muted, stifled, in the distance. Casey always took that as a sign of weakness, a timidity that rendered her powerless. Now, however, Mary, a woman liberated from the cruel bondage of authority, speaks unobstructedly. And Casey, for the first time, is listening. For her entire life, she has been missing her mother's voice. She hadn't realized that until now.

Casey opens the box and peers down at the Cross. The image on the front is scuffed from the impact with concrete, like a wound from war, a scar from the justifiable rage of a distraught daughter. She looks up at her mother, who is smiling, tears streaming down her cheeks. Then, like the bubble of revenge that burst when she stood in front of her father's grave, Casey's anger releases into the air.

She rises to her feet and wraps her arms around Mary, who returns the embrace. The two hold each other as if time had stood still. Then Casey chokes out the words that she hasn't spoken in years: "I love you, Mom."

"I love you, too," Mary replies.

Casey's eyes well up, and then a deluge of tears releases. "I've missed you so much," she says, sobbing, holding her mother tightly.

"I've missed you, too," Mary responds, squeezing her daughter close to her chest. "Welcome home."

Chapter 17

Back in the year 2000, Flooz.com was considered a colossal failure. And that assessment wasn't wrong—but only if you stop the story there. From our modern perspective, Flooz, as ill-conceived as it was, prepared the way for modern digital payment systems and virtual currencies like Venmo, PayPal, and Bitcoin. And, as history will eventually show us, these technologies, too, are merely the precursors to something else. The world is evolving, and failure has a funny way of teaching our species how to grow.

"Through death comes life," Mary told Casey on the phone the night of her father's funeral. "You have to trust that this is true."

IN MARY'S BACKYARD. MORNING.

Casey takes in her view of vibrant flowers surrounding dew-covered, lush green grass under the protective shade of white oak trees, the birds and trickling water supplying the melody to the rhythmic creaking chains of the porch swing. She takes a sip of tea. Mary is sitting beside her, resting her hand on her thigh. As Casey glances up at the sky and watches a morphing, wispy cloud float along, Mary speaks: "How did you sleep last night?"

"Like a fucking rock," Casey says with a smile.

Mary has never been entirely comfortable with her adult daughter's salty mouth, but she returns a laugh and says, "You know, Casey, since you're here, there's another thing I think you need to let go of. Something that will help you as you move forward." Casey redirects her eyes from the passing clouds to her mother. Mary has her full attention. "You need to release the anger you've had toward the God you've been led to believe in."

"I don't understand," Casey says. "Like, stop believing God exists? I've tried that already. I can't."

"No," Mary responds. "I mean that you've been angry at an Imitation God that's been taught to you, the distorted replica of the real one. And if you can release your misguided faith in that Imitation God, you will finally be able to see that the real one has been with you the whole time."

"I don't know what to believe," Casey says, once again staring at the clouds. "Everything I've ever known about God was shaped by Dad. Where does one end and the other begin? This is all so goddamn confusing."

"I don't know if making sense of everything is what's important right now," Mary responds. "There'll be a time for that. But there's one thing that will help you take your next step. It's the belief that God appears to us in the form of people, and through their love, we can know our maker. Jesus comes for us all, Casey. He just happens to look like someone who loves us."

Casey soaks in her mother's words, and Mary places her hand on top of Casey's. "We want to search out there for God, as if he's behind the scenes pulling invisible strings, governing world events, and selectively answering our prayers. But that's not the way God operates. God works through humans, coming for us when we need it most, comforting us when we are in pain, and guiding us toward our healing."

While Casey ponders what her mother is saying, she looks out at the pale blue sky peeking through the gray. Mary continues. "And we think that knowing God requires specific beliefs or the right identity. But you know that's not true."

Casey nods in agreement.

"The problem is, you also think that because you have rejected those beliefs, and no longer fit your former identity, that you are no longer in need of God," Mary says. "That's not true, either."

Casey turns her head and looks directly into Mary's eyes.

"Casey, you were made to meet your maker. And you can know them, not through the teaching of an authority, or the deciphering of events, but through the love of others. That's how God speaks. That's always how God has spoken. And that is the one belief you need to hold firmly as you begin your new life."

Casey propels the swing backward and lets gravity take it forward. "I've hated God for such a long time," she says. "I don't know if I can ever change that."

Mary grips Casey's hand. "You've hated God because you've been so certain that God hates you. But can't you see? God has been with you the entire time, even in your loss."

"Where?"

"Through the people who love you."

"Oh yeah? Like who?"

"Like your brother. Can't you see that?"

Casey's eyes squint.

"Dom's been there to encourage and support you during your time of need," Mary says. "He gave you a home when you lost yours, and he's been alongside you on your journey. You've been wondering where God is, Casey, but he's been riding next to you the whole way."

Casey's mind flashes an image of Dom in his sweat-stained DC hat, sitting in the passenger seat on a reluctant trip across America, listening to her rants, persevering through her combativeness, absorbing her pain, helping her move forward.

"Holy shit," she says, her eyes widening as she finally gets it. Her brother, an aimless misfit in her eyes, may not be as clueless as she thought he was.

"Dom is mourning, too," Mary says. "His experience has just been different from yours."

"Yeah, but it's been easier for him," Casey responds. "He didn't get stabbed in the heart by the sharp knife of fatherly rejection."

Mary looks at her with a sternness that Casey has not seen since she was a child. "He's experienced the pain of fatherly rejection, too, Casey. Very much so. It's just that his pain has come from the dull knife of inadequacy. He was never man enough for your father, and that has caused him immense anguish."

As if scales had fallen from her mind's eye, Casey is awakened to a side of her brother that had been hiding in plain sight. Dom didn't need to confront his father for abandoning him because he had never felt like he belonged in the first place. He has been silently grieving the absence of a dad his entire life. And Casey had never considered that, maybe, he had released any urge for vengeance long ago, if he ever had it, and has been moving forward in his own wise way.

"Holy shit," she repeats as she realizes that, because of her pain, she has been incapable of seeing her brother's.

"Dom has been there for you. The love of God in human form," Mary says. "And now, you need to return the gift. Let's get your Jeep, sweetie. It's time to go find your brother."

Chapter 18

At no point in his youth did Dominic King believe that his war hero father was proud to call him a son. From an early age, Dom tried to mimic Admiral King's every move and re-gurgitate everything he said to him, but even when Dom got it right, he never felt like it made a difference. By the time he reached the age of ten, Dom had learned that the best path forward was to simply say "Yes, sir" and try not to fuck up. But he did, a lot, and then faced the full brunt of his failings.

Mary, though, was always there to comfort Dom. This pro-voked Admiral King's ire, prompting him to erupt with accu-sations that she was "pussifying the boy" and "teaching him to be a limp-wristed nancy who can't handle the grizzly realities of life." Yet Mary shielded her child from his father's wrath, and she assured Dom that he would one day grow up to be a great man in his own way.

With a chronic sense of paternal abandonment, Dom looked up to his big sister, and, as the younger brother of Casey King, he was looking up at a bright star. She was his friend and role model, and when he was with Casey, he didn't feel alone. Even though she had a sisterly tendency to tease and trick him, and he was an easy target, he was there by her side until the day she left for college.

After his high school graduation, Dom moved out to California so he could be closer to her. Since Stanford apparently favors students with GPAs higher than 2.0 and whose application essays don't make statements like "it would be tight to kick it with my sis on campus", he enrolled at San Francisco State, which is only 30 miles north of Palo Alto. (The first person he met in the City by the Bay was a shaggy-haired kid from Pittsburgh named Phil, who moved to the West Coast with only an overstuffed suitcase packed with Grateful Dead t-shirts and an acoustic guitar. The two hit it off immediately.)

Dom made frequent visits to the Stanford campus and attended all of his sister's swim meets, sporting a tree costume and a large cardboard sign with things like "Casey Rules" scribbled on the front. He clipped every newspaper article she was in, absorbed every word she said to him, and looked up to her in every way.

After their father's funeral, Dom tried to follow Casey to Seattle, but she told him it was time to grow up and carve his own path. So he stayed in San Francisco to figure out how to do that. He made road trips to the Emerald City as often as he could get his shifts at T.G.I. Fridays covered, but by then, Casey was so focused on starting CityCart that Dom would spend his visits exploring the Puget Sound with Angie while Casey stayed in the apartment to code, analyze data, and sketch logos. On one such visit, Dom asked Casey if she wanted to go out and do something together after work, to which she snapped back, "I have important shit to do, Dom."

Dejected, he said goodbye to his sister, told her he couldn't wait to buy groceries online one day if he ever got a computer, grabbed his bag, and started the 800-mile trek back to San Francisco.

On the way back home, while stopping at a Shell station in Yreka, CA to purchase Red Bull and Doritos, he impulsively bought a lottery ticket.

AT AL'S AUTO IN ALEXANDRIA, VA. NOON.

Mary pulls into the parking lot and stops along the curb in front of the entrance to the auto repair shop. Casey looks at her mother and says in a soft voice, "I'm sorry I've ignored you for so long. You didn't deserve that."

"Love is patient," Mary replies. "I knew you'd respond in your time."

"I don't want to leave you now," Casey says.

"You know I'm always here for you," Mary replies. "And you can be with me whenever you want. But right now, your brother needs you more."

Casey hugs her mother with tears in her eyes, chokes out a thank you, and gets out of the car.

I-95 NORTH. PASSING BY PHILADELPHIA, PA. 2:45 PM.

The City of Brotherly Love's skyline glistens in the distance as the Jeep zooms up the interstate. Casey glances at the speedometer on the dash, then presses the accelerator.

ARRIVING AT THE JACOB JAVITZ CONVENTION CENTER. MANHATTAN. 4:30 PM.

The dented Jeep with a brand new radiator's brakes screech as its engine comes to a halt on the street. Casey springs from the vehicle, leaves her bag in the back, and runs toward the convention center. She does not expect Dom to still be here, but, as he once suggested to her, she is going to put her detective hat on to try and recreate his thought process. She comes up with two theories on what happened after she left him with the pigeons.

Theory one: Phil ditched his overbearing parents, depressed girlfriend, and three-year-old daughter, surprised Dom in NYC, and the two knuckleheads are somewhere in the East Village playing Dave Matthews songs on their guitars, only taking breaks to hug each other and say "I love you, bro."

Theory two: Dom went to an Ethiopian coffee shop and met a redheaded soccer player visiting from Minneapolis. She took him back home with her, and he's currently taking a bite of casserole while staring longingly into her hazel eyes.

Since neither of these theories is probable, Casey decides to take Dom's final suggestion and aimlessly search through the most populated city in America for someone who does not own a phone in the hopes that she will get lucky.

She walks laps through Manhattan's grid, determined to canvas every street in The Big Apple if she needs to, but then her pocket starts buzzing. She pulls her Nokia out and looks at the caller ID, which is displaying an unknown number with a 212 area code. She puts the device to her ear.

"Hello?" she says.

"Hey sis!" says Dom enthusiastically. "You back yet?"

"Yes! I'm somewhere in the East Village. I just walked past a venue called CBGB or GBCB or something like that. Wait, how did you know I was coming back to the city?"

"Mom called and told me."

"How did Mom get a hold of you?"

"I called her from my hotel when I checked in and gave her the number."

"Where are you?"

"The Plaza."

"Really?"

"Really. I got a room here. And room service. It's been siiiiick."

"Stay where you are, Dom," Casey says. "I'm coming for you."

AT THE PLAZA HOTEL. MIDTOWN MANHATTAN. 8:00 PM.

Casey knocks three times on the door of room 420. The door opens wide, and Dom, in a white bathrobe with ketchup stains on the chest, embraces her, lifts her up, and exclaims, "Caseyyyyyyyyy!" He puts her down, then picks her back up, then puts her down again.

"I'm sorry, Dom," she says, wasting no time. "For abandoning you. For letting my anger control my life and turn me against the people who have been there for me the whole time. Especially you. I've been a giant turd and you don't deserve that."

Dom gives her another tight hug. "I'm not just your brother in the good times, sis."

Casey's eyes well up. "I don't get how you've been able to put up with me. I've been wrong about everything."

"You haven't been wrong, Casey," Dom replies. "You've just been stopping the story short."

"Did you hear that from Mom?"

"Yeah. She told me to remind you of that. Hey, I have this room for another night. Want to go out and do something fun together?"

"Yes, Dom. Yes I do."

"Sick. First, I need to get my bag from the car. A bunch of pigeons shat all over me so I need another shirt. This bathrobe is super cozy, but I don't think any chicks will take me seriously."

Chapter 19

When Dom and Casey were young, Admiral King would often leave for extended periods to engage in Cold War naval operations. "The war is all around us, and the enemy is crouching in wait," he would tell his children before departing. "We must always stay vigilant."

During his absences, Mary was free to spread her wings around her children. One time, on a dark and stormy Texas night when Admiral King was overseas on a NATO exercise, Mary tucked her kids into bed. Thunder rumbled, and a tree branch swaying from the howling wind smacked against the window. A flash of lightning illuminated the bedroom.

"It's scary outside," four-year-old Dom said in a tiny voice, pulling his Star Wars blanket up to his Caesar-cut bangs.

"You're safe in here, my boy," Mary comforted her young son. "I'm with you. And you have your sister right beside you."

"When's Daddy coming home, Mommy?" Casey asked from her curled position next to Mary. "I miss him."

"It will be a little while, my girl," Mary said to her daughter. "But until then, you have me and your brother."

As the gentle snoring of a peaceful Dom began to emanate from the bed next to them, Mary ran her fingers through Casey's hair. The little girl snuggled in closer to her mother, then drifted into a deep sleep.

AT THE PLAZA HOTEL VALET. 11:00 AM.

The dented (but antler and mosquito-free) Jeep's brakes screech as its purring engine comes to a halt on the street. The valet springs from the vehicle, takes their bags, and puts them in the rear cargo space. Dom hands him a fifty.

The siblings buckle into the Jeep. Casey looks at her brother, his sweat-stained DC hat slightly crooked on his head, and smiles. He looks at his sister, her hair in its usual tight bun, and smiles back. Casey opens the center console and puts the mahogany box holding the Cross safely inside it.

"So where are we going?" Dom asks.

"I don't know," Casey says as she puts the bootlegged copy of Dave Matthews Band *Live at Red Rocks* into the CD drive. "Where do you want to go?"

Epilogue

I t was October of 2000. Here's a glimpse into what was going on back then.

SAN FRANCISCO, CA. 710 ASHBURY ST.
ON THE FIRST FLOOR. IN THE BEDROOM.

Casey King traces her finger along the glass of a framed picture of the 1997 Stanford Women's Swimming and Diving team hanging on her wall as the bay breeze wafts through her open window. Beneath it, prominently displayed in a mahogany box on the dresser, is the Cross. The sounds of an acoustic guitar pleasing the ghost of Jerry Garcia echo through the spacious Victorian home.

Her life, as she knows it now, is just beginning.

IN THE UNITED STATES

George Bush and Al Gore enter the final month of their quest for a job that would give them the power to press a button and start World War III, the fate of which rests in the hands of wrinkly, intoxicated septuagenarian golfers in Miami.

AROUND THE GLOBE

The Closing Ceremonies of the Sydney Olympics conclude, and the nations celebrate a brief time of peace before 2001 comes and all hell breaks loose.

ACROSS THE UNIVERSE

The universe containing 100 billion trillion stars spanning 93 billion light-years is expanding at 163,000 miles per hour, like it always is.

The events on the third planet orbiting one of the incomprehensible number of burning gas balls hurtling through the void are truly meaningful when you think about them from your perspective.

Author's Note

Thank you for reading this book. As a postscript, I want to offer a brief commentary on it. If you're the type of reader who likes to come to your own conclusions about a book's meaning, then I'd suggest skipping this note. If, however, you appreciate authorial explanation, then read on.

As a teacher, Jesus' preferred method was to convey his lessons through short, relatable stories called parables. Parables are not just illustrations. For Jesus, they were the primary vehicle through which he dismantled his audience's worldview and replaced it with the true meaning of the kingdom of God. Through parables, Jesus turned his audience's beliefs upside down. Or, in actuality, he turned them right side up by subverting expectations and rearranging their spiritual furniture.

I chose to write *The Parable of the Road* to make a point about reimagining Christianity, especially for those whose faith was shaped by the evangelical church. As with Jesus' parables, the characters are representatives.

Casey embodies post-evangelicals who were once entirely devoted to their faith, then got deeply wounded, and now are consumed by anger. Casey, like many of us, feels abandoned and betrayed by the authorities she loved dearly. As a result of egregious religious abuse, people like Casey have lost their framework for understanding the world, and as a result, reject God and regret their past.

Dom represents post-evangelicals who never truly fit the system they were raised in, have moved beyond the faith of their childhood, and are figuring out their path while displaying the dedicated love of God through their actions, ironically contrary to many who claim to follow Jesus. Dom is a true saint.

Admiral King represents the authoritarian religious structures that teach a vindictive God, create rigid beliefs and rules, and then turn on anything and anyone that doesn't fit. Admiral King is powerful, awe-inspiring, and incapable of change. He is an adversarial force, one who continues to haunt from the past.

Mary, on the other hand, represents the true love of God, the comfort of the Spirit, and the healing work of Jesus. Constrained by authoritative structures, her voice is stifled. But, once freed, speaks with power to those who will listen. She is a hero and a guide.

The Cross, obviously the central symbol of the Christian faith, is an emblem of redemption in this story. Whereas evangelicalism gives it a truncated, counterfeit meaning of salvation through divine punishment, the Cross is a much richer symbol of our holistic liberation from evil. On the other side of a deconstructed faith, it can be seen as a symbol of our transformation—the death of our old lives, and the beginning of our new ones. Accepting the Cross in this truer and better picture, rather than rejecting it altogether, is the best way to say "fuck you" to the institutions that have distorted its meaning.

The point of this book, to put it on the nose, is that the evangelical faith is dead for many. It provided a simplistic view of God and life that doesn't hold up to scrutiny. There is no returning to it. And that, rightfully so, produces a mixture of sadness and anger, a consuming grief that spawns a relentless thirst for revenge against those who have abused religious power. But revenge is not the answer, nor is it possible. And neither is rejecting Christianity altogether. The faith has always been bigger than any tradition that claims it, and the only way to see this is to move beyond its institutionalized corruption and into the true experience of God.

For those who have left evangelicalism, the way forward is to write a new story, one that transcends the narrative of our discarded former belief system. God is still real and present, and the voice of the Spirit, liberated from the shackles of reductive theology, can now speak. Humans, rather than doctrines or organizations, are the true conduit of God's love. This has always been, and will forever be, true.

If those of us who have left the church can confront our grief and release our blinding anger, we can see that the journey through evangelicalism, as painful as it was, is not a waste. It has prepared us to encounter God in deeper, more meaningful ways.

New life *is* possible, but only if we move forward in a resurrected faith with the Spirit as our guide. And to do this, we need our brothers and sisters.

They're all around us. I hope you find them.

Acknowledgements

There are so many beautiful souls to thank for their role in creating *The Parable of the Road*.

My parents hosted me at their home in Lake Almanor, CA, and witnessed me feverishly type the first draft over a long weekend. They made sure I took short breaks to eat and interact with the real world. So thank you, Mom and Dad, for your care. I was able to finish the first draft in a beautiful setting without starving or losing my mind.

The first draft sucked, though, as they always do. My wife, Lisa, read the initial manuscript and provided insight that radically transformed the book as you know it. Writing this was an iterative process, and Lisa was the chief editor through each evolutionary stage. So thank you, my red-headed soccer player from Minneapolis, for your dedication and support.

When it came time to test the novel and see if it was worth publishing, my beta readers gave me feedback that helped me discover what was working, what wasn't, and how the book might be received. So thank you to Marie Fox, Garrett McGeein, Alison Berreman, Josh Drabik, Allison Siegmann, Ben Ragains, Jenn Nicholson, and Melanie Gregory for your input and inspiration.

As a first-time author, I expected to self-publish. But then I discovered SacraSage Press. Their team, especially Jonathan Foster, made this book come alive. Jonathan also provided developmental editing, which shaped this story in deeper, better ways. Thank you, SacraSage.

And, finally, thank you to *you*, whoever you are, for reading this novel. It's been said that the moment you publish a book, it belongs to the reader. Well, here you go. Shalom.

Brandon